Opening
to
Abundance

A 31-Day Process of Self-Discovery

Pathwork Publications

The Pathwork of Self-Transformation
Eva Pierrakos
Bantam 1990. ISBN 0-553-34896

Fear No Evil, *The Pathwork Method of Transforming the Lower Self*
Eva Pierrakos and Donovan Thesenga
Pathwork Press, 1993 ISBN 0-9614777-2-5

Creating Union, *The Essence of Intimate Relationship,*
2nd Edition
Eva Pierrakos and Judith Saly
Pathwork Press, 2002. ISBN 0-9614777-8-4

The Undefended Self, *Living the Pathwork,*
3rd Edition
Susan Thesenga
Pathwork Press, 2001. ISBN 0-9614777-7-6

Surrender to God Within, *Pathwork at the Soul Level*
Eva Pierrakos and Donovan Thesenga
Pathwork Press, 1997. ISBN 0-9614777-5-x

Complete Lectures of the Pathwork, *In Two Editions*
Eva Pierrakos
CD-ROM version
Pathwork Press, 2000. ISBN 0-9614777-6-8

Opening to Abundance, *A 31-Day Process of Self-Discovery*
Charles Cresson Wood
Pathwork Press, 2004. ISBN 0-9614777-9-2

Pathwork Press, P.O. Box 6010, Charlottesville, VA 22906
1-800-728-4967; email: pathworkpress@pathwork.org;
www.pathwork.org

Opening
to
Abundance

A 31-Day Process of Self-Discovery

By Charles Cresson Wood
Based on material by Eva Broch Pierrakos

Pathwork Press
Charlottesville, Virginia
2004

PRINTED IN THE UNITED STATES OF AMERICA
10 09 08 07 06 05 04   10 9 8 7 6 5 4 3 2 1

Library of Congress Cataloging-in-Publication Data

Library of Congress Cataloging-in-Publication Data

Wood, Charles Cresson.
  Opening to abundance : a 31-day process of self-discovery / by Charles Cresson Wood ; based on material by Eva Broch Pierrakos.
      p. cm.
  Includes bibliographical references.
  ISBN 0-9614777-9-2 (alk. paper)
  1. Success--Religious aspects. I. Pierrakos, Eva, 1915-1979. II. Title.

  BL65.S84W66 2004
  204'.4--dc22

                              2004009541

Pathwork Guide Quotes used throughout text with permission from The Pathwork Foundation.
Cover Art: Rassouli, Freydoon. *The Messiah*
          www.Rassouli.com
Author Photo: Pol Stafford
Book Design and Production: Lisa Willow

Contents

Introduction

This book is intended to remind you that you can always change your attitudes and perspectives about life, even if you believe you have very little control over your current circumstances. Many people make the error of believing that the circumstances of their lives are more important than their state of mind. To the contrary, all things on earth originate in the world of consciousness. In other words, when we change our state of mind, then the world around us changes as well.

While we have much more power to change the circumstances of our lives than we give ourselves credit for, whether we give ourselves permission to be happy is ultimately a function of our internal state. It is not a function of the circumstances of our lives. This permission can only be gained by becoming aware of, and later transforming, the many layers of our consciousness. It is this process of becoming aware of our inner state, of transforming our many layers of consciousness, that we will address in this book.

If you have been wrestling with issues related to abundance, or if in some other way you have been wrestling with manifesting the life you desire, this book will empower you to make constructive changes. It doesn't matter how much money you have, it doesn't matter how successful you have been in your career, and it doesn't matter how well you have done in love. Everyone can expand their capacity to create desirable circumstances by transforming their consciousness.

This book is also intended to help generate a widespread discussion about the spiritual underpinnings associated with the manifestation of abundance. I strongly believe that through the process of discovering and revealing our deepest truths, through the removal of our self-imposed barriers to experiencing the life we want, through the development of faith in the benign nature of life on earth, and through the resulting ability to relax ego control, we all can manifest the life we want both creatively and abundantly. The Pathwork material provides very specific and practical instructions for doing just this. This book offers a sampling of these profound teachings.

On another note, this book is meant to be savored slowly. If you read it quickly, you will miss the most important part, which involves taking the time to go deep within yourself to investigate how these ideas could be applied to your life. To really get value, to really change your life, you must work on the questions at the end of each chapter. So if you intended to read the whole book in a single day, the author strongly advises that you abandon your original plan and instead take your time. The book is written so that you can read a single chapter (day 1 through 31) each day for a one-month period.

The chapters of this book are sequenced in such a way that they build on the chapters that come earlier. In addition, a subtle and profound shift in abundance consciousness is often the result of immersing yourself in this material for a considerable period of time. For these reasons, the author recommends that the chapters be read in the sequence in which they are presented. Alternatively, if there is a particular aspect of creating abundance that you are interested in right now, you may consult the table of contents to identify the chapter that speaks to this same concern. If you choose this alternative approach, you are urged to read the chapters in numerical order later. So that the material in this book can best sink into your unconscious mind, to allow the deeper levels of your being to be engaged with abundance issues, I suggest you combine two or more of the following approaches to the material in this book:

Read a chapter right after waking up in the morning,
Read a chapter right before going to sleep at night,
Read a chapter immediately before your meditation,
Read a chapter right before writing in your personal
    journal, and/or
Read a chapter right before going into extended prayer.

For best results, ask for God and the higher forces within you to guide you immediately before you begin one of the activities mentioned above. Also be sure to keep some paper and a writing instrument nearby to record the new ideas that come to you.

Each of the stories in this book is meant to illustrate the main ideas found in the accompanying quote. The stories are also intended to prompt you to think about how these concepts could manifest in your own life. All the stories are the true personal experiences of people I know. The experiences of the individuals described in the stories are neither miraculous nor extraordinary. These same experiences are all readily available to you.

The questions at the end of each chapter are intended to assist you in applying the concepts to your own life. You are urged to notice which of these five questions intrigues you. You can then let the other questions temporarily drop away from your conscious mind. If more than one question in a chapter speaks to you, by all means stay with that chapter as long as you continue to get new insights.

These questions can be viewed as a menu at a large Chinese restaurant. These menus have many items, including some items you never heard of before and some items you can't imagine. At a Chinese restaurant you can't eat everything all at once, so you pick only those things that seem most to suit you in the moment. So it should be with these questions. Don't try to understand everything immediately. Take what you can handle right now, and let the rest simply exist, perhaps to be sampled and digested at some time in the future.

As the Chinese restaurant example implies, you are urged to read this book several times, as long as something in the book continues to speak to you. Each time you read the book your consciousness will be different, your circumstances will be different, and your understanding of life will be different. If you allow God and the higher forces within you to work through you, each time you read this book you can gain new insights about your current circumstances. Allow this book to help open you to the truth of your life, and let this deeper truth come forward into your conscious mind.

Conducting an Abundance Consciousness Litmus Test

Exactly where do you stand when it comes to your own abundance? For example, is there part of you that is afraid of happiness? Is there another part of you that is in despair and hopelessness? Is there yet another part of you that feels disempowered and ineffectual? Or perhaps you feel delightfully connected with the events of your life, welcoming each one as a gift from the world of spirit? Perhaps you deeply understand the cause and effect of many events and situations in your life? Perhaps you open to experiencing all of your feelings, knowing that by accepting the truth, you discover your own freedom? Whatever your present state of abundance consciousness, this chapter will discuss a practical and always-applicable tool. The tool happens to be built into your psyche, so you never need to be worried about not having it when you need it.

According to the Pathwork material, whenever you feel anything less than joyous, free, uninhibited, expansive, and fulfilled, you are operating with some sort of spiritual error. In other words, in these circumstances you are violating a spiritual law. In many cases people do not want to acknowledge this spiritual error, and in many other cases people are not even consciously aware of such an error. This book is specifically intended to assist you with the identification and clarification of these errors, and then later with the correction of these errors.

The Pathwork material also says that you cannot use your innate power to create on matters outside of yourself unless you have first come to terms with what is inside of yourself. And your feelings and emotions are a reliable barometer telling you what needs attention, where you are in illusion, where you are not in truth, and so forth. Your power to create the life you want will be expanded as you master your own inner world.[1][*] As long as you have not mastered yourself, as long as you have not yet come to terms with the destructive and unevolved parts of yourself, you cannot be aligned with Divine consciousness. To the extent that you align with Divine consciousness, you can open to limitless possibilities, pleasure supreme, as well as meaningful expansion and experience.

As you come to terms with the destructive and unevolved parts of yourself, you will also come to appreciate how you have created your own life. So by looking at your feelings and emotions, by working on your personal issues, you will be shown how cause and effect operate in your own life. As your consciousness is raised through this process, you will see connections that were not previously evident.[2] An understanding of cause and effect naturally leads to confidence and faith in the life process. As confidence and faith are enhanced, you will take on greater self-responsibility.

As you are increasingly able to see the truth, as you are increasingly able to correct those parts of yourself that are in opposition to spiritual law, you will come to appreciate how much freedom you have. This will help you to drop victimization, blame, and other behaviors that deny your responsibility for creating the life you want.[3] Along with this will go a new ability to clearly see what is your

---

[1] See Pathwork Guide Lecture 141
[*] The parenthetical Pathwork references provided throughout this book are explained in the chapter titled "Researching Specific Lecture References."
[2] See Pathwork Guide Lecture 245
[3] See Pathwork Guide Lecture 171

own responsibility and what is the responsibility of others. This healthy balance will allow you not only to establish satisfying relationships, but also to truly create the life you so ardently seek. This balance and openness will help you to receive the abundance and support you have been blocking and resisting.

If you continue to use the Pathwork material, you will also come to terms with the ways your legitimate needs as a child were not fulfilled. As you deeply feel the pain of these unmet needs, as you understand the origins of this pain, you will come to appreciate that you have been pursuing false needs to compensate for the lack of fulfillment in childhood. For example, a child needs to be taken care of; it needs solely to receive the care of others. But an adult who was not sufficiently taken care of as a child may continue to seek the perfect parents who could do this. While the need to receive this type of care was a real need for a child, it is a false need for an adult. An adult who pursues such a false need will be frustrated and unfulfilled.[4] When adults understand how this works in their own lives, they can devote their energies to the fulfillment of their real needs, such as rewarding relationships, self-expression, spiritual development, and making a contribution to life.

With this brief background about the Pathwork process in mind, as an exercise, you are invited to make a list of all the areas where you are dissatisfied with your life. This exercise may take an hour, or you may want to stretch it out over a few days. After you have completed the list, see whether there are similar issues occurring in more than one area. For example, not feeling confident to speak up about your needs might affect not only your

---

[4] See Pathwrok Guide Lecture 192

relationship with your spouse, but also your relationships at work. See whether you can detect any other
similarities across your life. This is the starting point for
your own deep inner process to identify and change
those things that hold you back. The deeper you take this
process, the more rewarding the search will be, and the
more you will have empowering new insights into both
your life task and your current circumstances.[5] This book
is intended to support you in going deeper into this
vitally important area.

[5] See Pathwork Guide Lecture 124

Understanding the Power of Your Beliefs

"You must know and believe that you have the right and the ability to mold and create substance with your mind. You may never have even thought of this possibility, so now when you examine your attitude, you may find that you strongly doubt that you can do it. Accept this possibility as a hypothesis to begin with, until you know that it is indeed true." *(Pathwork Guide Lecture194)*

Affirmation

I intend to evolve my consciousness, and I thereby create a new energy field that opens new possibilities; I feel how this is distinctly different from holding onto the same state of consciousness, which reinforces the way things have been.

Brock's Story

Feeling discouraged about the future, Brock really didn't know what he wanted to do when he grew up, even though he was nineteen and a sophomore in college. A friend gave him a magazine article that discussed a previously unknown high-tech problem. Immediately fascinated with the problem, Brock believed this issue would become very important in the years ahead. He held no hope of ever working in this area, because it wasn't even viewed as a legitimate specialty and because there weren't even job titles for those who might work on these matters. While he continued with college, Brock maintained his keen interest in the area by reading a variety of related articles. After graduation from college, he went to work for an accounting firm but found the work dry and uninteresting. Returning to graduate school full time, he pursued two master's degrees. At this point he did everything he could to work on this exciting and emerging area. He did part-time consulting for a nearby bank on this matter and also wrote project reports and his master's thesis on this same topic. He still held no hope of working in the field, because there were no jobs of this type available. A few months before graduation, Brock was reading the help wanted section of the *Wall Street Journal.* He was surprised to see an advertisement for a job at a prestigious research institute, a job in the field he had been so ardently pursuing. The ad stated that applicants must have 10 years of experience in the field and ideally a Ph.D. Although he had neither of these qualifications, he sent his sparse résumé to the research institute. He was surprised when they called to request an interview by phone. He was even more surprised to have them flying him across the country for a second interview. Brock was floored when he visited the institute and discovered that the hiring manager was the same person who wrote the article that had first piqued his interest several years earlier. A few weeks later, he was elated to get a job offer that would allow him to work under and be mentored by this same man, the most famous researcher in the field. He accepted the offer without hesitation. Twenty-two years after that, Brock is still grateful that he is able to work on a topic that once was his hobby.

Questions for Meditation and Journal Work

1. Could you approach the unfulfilled areas of your life with an attitude of open-minded experimentation as well as a willingness to have your faith grow as results are demonstrated?

2. Can you seriously believe that your life could be different than it is today? Or are you convinced that it must continue to be as it is now? Do you have the courage to believe that life can be the way you long for it to be?

3. Create a vivid and compelling visualization of the life you so ardently desire. What are the specific components of this visualization?

4. If your world is not showing up the way you consciously want it to, could there be a "no" in your subconscious mind that opposes the conscious "yes"? If so, what might that "no" be?

5. Can you imagine that every situation in your life—positive or negative—is the result of words you have spoken, or perhaps still are speaking on some level deep within yourself?

Day 2

Owning Your Ability to Create

"You have no idea how strong your own spirit is. You constantly underestimate and believe yourself to be much weaker and much more ineffectual than you actually are. Since you must experience according to your belief, it is difficult to find how strong you really are. You can create anything, for you have all Divine creative forces at your disposal. And of course you do exactly that. Some of your creations are undesirable, springing from negative beliefs and distorted notions. If you could only see the immense power that dwells in your thoughts, your beliefs, your attitudes, and your desires!" (Pathwork Guide Lecture 254)

Affirmation

I now more deeply unify and align the divided parts of myself, and as a result, I am beginning to more deeply experience my own great creative power.

Hazel's Story

Eleven years ago, after a messy divorce, Hazel was broke and utterly discouraged about her future. She didn't feel like she had any room to breathe financially. One day she received a chain letter promising thousands of dollars if she sent only one dollar to the person on the top of the list, added her name to the bottom of the list, and then forwarded the list to 100 other people. Their "suggestion" was to use mail-order labels for this purpose. Even though chain letters are illegal, in her desperation she ordered 500 labels instead of 100. All together she spent $350 that she didn't really have to spare. While she waited for her labels to arrive, she busied herself photocopying a new version of the letter, purchasing stamps, and stuffing envelopes. Every day she waited for the solution to all her financial problems to arrive in the mail, becoming increasingly obsessed about exactly how much she would receive. A sum of $30,000 seemed guaranteed, even at the smallest 1 percent response level. As the days passed, she realized that a one-time payment of $30,000 would not really change her life—that what she needed was a reliable and constant source of income. She saw that she had been looking for a magical solution, looking for some force outside herself to rescue her. She then came to appreciate that the mass-mailing label company had probably been the source of the letter. By that point she noticed that not even one dollar of this scheme had come to her, and probably not one dollar ever would. She decided to get realistic, to take self-responsibility, and to challenge the part of herself that believed in a fantasy world with successful chain letters. She decided to do whatever was necessary. She has kept this important lesson in mind every day for the last 11 years, and she has worked hard and gone on to create her own manufacturing business and then sell it to her employees. The business still provides her with a regular annual income, even though she has since moved on to other pursuits, which by the way have also been surprisingly successful, again because she was willing to do whatever was necessary. But she still takes self-responsibility, still asks herself what is realistic and reasonable, and still leaves a special allowance for unanticipated events. People perceive her to be rich, but her real source of wealth is her creative power.

Questions for Meditation and Journal Work

1. Entertain the possibility that you have an abundant amount of creative power at your disposal. Can you believe, with God's help, that you can use this creative power to overcome any hurdle or limitation?

2. Consider that what you have or do not have in this life is a direct result of what you think, what you feel, and what you want. Additionally consider that your life is a result of both your consciousness and your unconsciousness. With this as a background, what part of you is blocking the manifestation you so ardently desire?

3. Consider the possibility that you are not your ego consciousness. That is to say you are not an isolated or separate fragment of consciousness. Consider that you instead are an integrated and important part of God's creation. If indeed this is true, wouldn't you have vast and untapped powers to create the life you desire?

4. In your mind's eye, see yourself as a manifestation of God. See yourself as a channel for God's creative power. See how the manifestations of this power are entirely up to you, because God has given you free will. How does this feel?

5. Consider that your power to create has a governor or limiting mechanism on it. Consider that this power to create is limited so long as there are parts of yourself that need purification. Consider that God created life this way so that you would not unduly damage other people and other aspects of the world with these same destructive and unevolved aspects of yourself. Are you willing and ready to transform these destructive and unevolved parts of yourself so that your power to create may then be enhanced?

Adopting an Intention to Change

"Ask a concise question of your innermost being: 'What approach can I use to live my life without a pretense? How does it feel to bring forth better ways of responding to life's experiences?' In answer to these questions, something new will evolve; . . . healthy, resilient, adequate, truthful reactions will come from your real nature, which does not need to be concealed. In this re-creating process, formulate your sentences very concisely. State that what you do does not work and why it does not work, and that you wish to operate in a different way. These sentences, if they are meant, have great creative power. They can be meant, they must be meant, when you fully comprehend the harm you are doing by remaining in your old attitudes." (Pathwork Guide Lecture 176)

Affirmation

I commit to re-creation of my life, so that it is a reflection both of my desire to live authentically and an expression of my deepest soul yearnings.

Phil and Eve's Story

A married couple, Phil and Eve, lived in a posh suburb just outside a very large and affluent city. A former president of the country and his wife lived close to their house. Phil and Eve had just moved into their own large custom dream house on two acres of land. They had three children: two in elementary school and one in middle school. The children were sent to one of the finest private schools in the country. Phil had a "good job" with a well-known think tank in that same swank suburb. In the essence of those times (about 1970), as they saw it, Phil and Eve had "made it." One day Phil came home and without any fanfare announced he had quit his job. He said he couldn't stand the rat race any longer. Eve was precipitously thrown into a very fearful state. She worried that they were going to lose everything; she worried that they would not be able to take care of the kids. She was anxious and despairing about what was going to happen next. After the shock of it all subsided, they sold the house, moved to the country, and through their own diligent and dedicated efforts became successful artisans. Although they never had as much income as they did before, their lives turned out to be fuller and richer in every way. For example, being self-employed allowed them to devote a significant amount of their time to their own spiritual development. Through this change in circumstances, they came to appreciate that there was nothing ennobling in affluence, and at the same time, nothing demeaning in poverty. They also came to see how there is God's all-pervading and everlasting grace, which falls upon us all, no matter what our financial circumstances may be.

Questions for Mediation and Journal Work

1. In the story, were Phil and Eve originally successful, or were they successful in the end? How did their concept of success change over time? Exactly what does success mean to you now? Will this concept sustain you 10, 20, 30 years into the future?

2. Try to formulate a clear and concise intention to change your life. Can you see and feel how this new life would allow your positive, healthy, and life-supporting self to manifest? Can you see how this new life would help you to give up destructive and life-negating patterns?

3. When it comes to changing your life, are appearances more important than the truth? If so, how much of your life substance are you willing to sacrifice in order to paint a picture that is untrue?

4. Consider that as long as your self-will is placed in a more important position than God's will, you will never know the certainty of God's abundance. With this in mind, are you willing to let go of who you thought you were, or who you thought you had to be, in order to embrace the truth of who you really are (a Divine manifestation of God)?

5. Are you willing and resolved to working your way out of the maze of your own negative creations and negative illusions? If so, the first step is to find, acknowledge, and accept your own negative attitudes, destructive feelings, subtle lies, intention to cheat, and life-defeating resistance to good feelings. Once you have come to terms with your own negative creations, the second step is to see how you like these negative creations, how you find pleasure in them. Once you discover this pleasure, you will also see how it keeps you stuck.

Overcoming Fear of Movement

"When you observe your negative visualization—it exists at first only on an unconscious level and later perhaps on a semiconscious level—you will see that your fear of movement translates into the message, 'If I move, what will come will be worse, so I better stay where I am.' Challenge this message that comes out from a corner of your hidden being. Challenge it and replace it with the truth that, as a result of your total giving and commitment to the movement of your innermost being, of your path, you can rightfully claim the universe's abundance. In the spirit of total devotion, total commitment of giving all of yourself to life, you will find it not so difficult to feel deserving, to know that only better can come." (Pathwork Guide Lecture 241)

Affirmation

I now let go of that heavy and resistant part of me that is firmly holding onto the way things have been; I feel my fear but choose to trust the changes that life brings.

Connie's Story

Connie met Jim at a local meeting of a spiritual group and right away felt a significant, although somewhat scary, attraction to him. Jim felt the same way about Connie. They went on a few dates together and enjoyed each other's company and friendship, but both were afraid to get into a serious relationship. Connie found excuses to avoid her fear of rejection by rationalizing that he probably was not interested in her in "that way." She felt safe if she did not have to think of the possibility of rejection. Connie was recently divorced and still healing from the trauma of that experience. Jim didn't want to get into another relationship unless he knew it was right. He had experienced several relationships where he had held back his loving feelings but had not realized that he was the only one who could change that withholding. They shared the same circle of friends, and as a result they both were concerned about how awkward things might be at future spiritual group meetings if they were to break up after having been serious. There were other considerations, but at first they were both reluctant to speak about them. One evening, after being very much aware of a powerful force between them, as well as their desire to pursue a romantic relationship, they sat with each other and discussed all their fears about becoming more deeply involved. After hearing each other out, they both realized they had free will, that they could step over the threshold of fear. They affirmed that they were both self-responsible adults and could handle any outcome. Both of them realized that they would never know what could have been if they didn't take a risk. After making the decision to let go, the energy and power of the eros between them was amazing.

The feelings of joy and excitement of being together and sharing themselves carried with it all the strength to go deeper and become more intimate. From that point on they let themselves open to what was meant to be, and even though some aspects of relationship continued to bring up fears and uncertainties, they looked at their feelings, worked through their distorted beliefs and misconceptions, and came from a very honest and committed place. They went on to discover deeper aspects of themselves through intimate relationship, and also to discover the magnificence of the soul of their partner.

Connie and Jim got married soon thereafter and now have a rich and fulfilling relationship. Their relationship is not without problems, but their commitment to movement and expansion grounds them in the potential of love's abundance.

Questions for Meditation and Journal Work

1. Can you connect to that deeper part of your soul that yearns for expansion, movement, and change? When you do, feel how your self-expression is fostered by movement and change. Feel how your fear of change prevents your self-expression.

2. Is there some part of you that believes only an unchanging situation is secure? In this part of you, does change lead to the unknown, and is it therefore to be feared?

3. Imagine that both life and the universe are trustworthy, beautiful, desirable, and secure. Imagine that you therefore trust the unknown future. What would you do differently if indeed you inhabited this reality?

4. Can you deliberately and intentionally envision change as a desirable, joyful, and necessary aspect of life, as the necessary process of creating the abundance for which you yearn?

5. Can you feel how psychically and spiritually boxed in you are when you do not allow yourself to have movement and change? Can you feel how you are doing the equivalent of holding your breath? Is this really the way you want to live?

Letting Go of Control

"Letting go is giving. Movement is therefore a substantial part of love and trust. Do you not notice that when you are in an ungiving state of mind, you cannot receive anything, even if it is right at your doorstep, ready to enrich you? You do not perceive it, or if you do, you misunderstand it and miss out on it, and so it passes you by."

(Pathwork Guide Lecture 241)

Affirmation

I am now reeducating that part of me that erroneously believes I will be safer and richer if I hold back and if I hold on.

Rudolph's Story

Rudolph was a psychologist and a spiritual counselor in his early thirties. While it was not unusual for him to have worries about money, at this time of his life, the number of active clients he had was rapidly dwindling. Because this was his only source of income, this development made him very scared. He felt his practice drying up, and this picture gripped him in a compelling way. He prayed about this problem and received some very clear guidance. The guidance was exactly the opposite of what he expected. He expected to get a new strategy for generating money. What he got were instructions to give money to two friends of his who were in worse financial shape than he was. Rudolph understood that he needed to give them what he was holding onto so tightly. Immediately after his prayers, although it was very difficult, he went to his checkbook and wrote them both a check. After that, his whole world turned around. At that moment, he felt saved, elated, and trusting of life. The number of clients he saw also increased soon thereafter. The same phenomenon happened while he was running a long and difficult race, soon after the previous incident. Near the end of the race, he was in great pain, and he prayed for assistance to make it through to the end. He received guidance that he should encourage those around him who were also in pain. After he urged his fellow runners on, he received a large and sustaining surge of energy to finish the race. In both instances, Rudolph was giving others what he felt he didn't have. In both instances he trusted the flow of life, instead of trying to control the situation and outwit his fear.

Questions for Meditation and Journal Work

1. Consider that your involuntary internal processes, such as the pumping of your blood, are self-regulating. Consider that your intuition and other spiritual involuntary processes are also self-regulating. With an overactive self-will, are you blocking the natural movement of these spiritual involuntary processes?

2. Are you attempting to exercise control over an aspect of your life that is, in reality, not directly controllable? Wouldn't you be happier if you let go of this attempt to force something that is not under your direct control?

3. Are you afraid of not being in control over your life? Do you see how this tense insistence on maintaining control prevents you from being in peace and prevents you from having confidence in life? Can you instead accept your limitations and open to support from places other than your conscious mind?

4. Is there part of you that is energetically tight, a part that defends against and rejects new ideas? Can you see how this approach to life can block the information that could turn your life around?

5. Is there part of you that doesn't want to admit that for every advantage there is a disadvantage, for every benefit you enjoy there is a price? Can you relax into this aspect of reality rather than insisting that you not suffer the disadvantage, or that you not pay the price?

Committing to Follow Divine Will

"Many of your conflicts are very simply a result of your fear of commitment. . . . You are afraid of making a mistake when you have a choice, so you vacillate, not taking a full stand. This is the inner weakness and lack of backbone that now also manifests on an outer level. The only way you can be sure that a choice is the right one at any given time is to completely surrender to the will of God and trust Divine guidance." (Pathwork Guide Lecture 257)

Affirmation

I bring my entire consciousness—my physical self, my mental self, and my emotional self— into alignment with God's will. To achieve this end, I open myself to being fluid and flexible on all levels.

Chris's Story

Chris had been diligently working in the computer field for many years. He had a small business that sold software he had written. With three employees, the firm never seemed to grow; it just stayed about the same size year after year. About this same time Chris started to become more deeply involved with his own spiritual work. He wondered whether his firm was a gift from God, intended to provide the means for him to more avidly pursue his spiritual work. Shortly thereafter he retained a business coach to help him expand the business so that he could later sell it. The coach was an ex-policeman who wasn't willing to play games—from Chris he wanted the straight truth and total commitment to results. Although at first it was a bit scary, the work with his coach shook up and reinvigorated Chris's business in a way he had never anticipated. Revenues and profits expanded significantly. Chris came to see how he had a variety of misconceptions and negative intentions that were at cross purposes with his more conscious intention to grow and later sell the business. For example, he had the misconception that he needed to pamper his employees and that they would quit if he did not. In keeping with this viewpoint, the performance of his employees had lagged way behind what they were capable of delivering. These misconceptions and negative intentions prevented Chris from fully committing to the success of his business. Later, with his work on the business aided by the coach, Chris came to appreciate that what his business was doing was good and right for all people concerned. Just after that, he prayed to hear the authentic voice of God inside him, to discern whether this guidance was indeed in the service of a higher good for him, his employees, and all others concerned. He came to understand that indeed the guidance was consistent with Divine will, and he felt a new sense of personal integration. This new alignment of purpose allowed him to feel good about the business, to utterly commit to having it become successful.

A few months after that he received and accepted a generous offer to sell his business to another firm. After negotiating severance packages worth six month's of pay for all of his former employees, Chris used the proceeds from the sale to go still more deeply into his own spiritual work, an endeavor he then felt was deeply aligned with God's will.

Questions for Meditation and Journal Work

1. Are you willing to consider that the abundance you have received, as well as the abundance you may soon receive, are intended to support you in doing your spiritual work?

2. Although you may consciously be committed to God's will, on deeper levels there are likely to be parts of you that are not so committed. Unless you acknowledge the parts of you that don't intend to be in alignment with God's will, your conscious intention will be thwarted and blocked. So that you can avoid self-deception, so that you can gain proper discernment, ask yourself in prayer what parts of you might not want to align with God's will.

3. What would your effort to create abundance look like if you were utterly, wholeheartedly, and fully committed to both love and truth (in other words, committed to God's will)?

4. Are you willing to so utterly commit yourself to God's will that you can see every aspect of your current life as right and perfect, as a reflection of your inner state, and as a gift assisting you with your spiritual evolution?

5. How is it that having your desired fulfillment may also be moving you one step closer to God? How is it that your desired fulfillment may in some way be advancing your spiritual evolution?

Rebalancing Giving and Receiving

"To the degree you offer generously and trustingly the best you have to give to life, allowing God to take over, to that very same degree will you feel perfectly entitled to spread your arms wide to receive the best life has to offer."

(Pathwork Guide Lecture 212)

Affirmation

I give the very best of myself, with the intention to positively and constructively influence everything and everyone around me.

Joanna's Story

At the age of 40, Joanna married the man of her dreams and had two children in the next five years. At that time she was working as a psychotherapist in private practice, and she felt abundant financially, emotionally, and spiritually. She says she will never forget the moment when her life dramatically turned around. Just three years earlier, her life was quite different and looking very bleak. Joanna had moved to New York City after a series of failed relationships. Unable to find work in the field of psychology, and her savings exhausted, she found herself taking any job. In this case it was work as a secretary, where she barely made enough to live on. She felt humiliated because she had to accept the job, and every day before she went to the office, she cried and raged in her bathroom. She was also disappointed because she longed to have a husband and family. She was in a relationship, but the man did not want to commit to her and she saw her biological clock winding down.

Desperate, embarrassed, depressed, and poor, she finally took to heart the need to see where she was cheating life, where she was holding back her best, and therefore not receiving the best life had to offer. Because she was contemptuous of her job and the people she worked with, she felt that the workplace was a good place to start. Instead of racing sloppily through her work, she committed to doing her best every moment on every task she was given. The next day she stayed in the office when everyone else went to lunch to retype a letter three times until it was perfect. (This took place before personal computers were widely used.) In the quiet office she felt the tears start again when she thought about the ways her life did not match her dreams. In spite of her sorrow, she reaffirmed her intention to give her best, no matter what. A few minutes later, she looked up to see the president of the company standing at her desk, offering her a raise and a promotion because "unnamed colleagues" had been praising her work and her capacities. She was astonished. Six months later she was promoted again and could then care for herself in a decent way. Despite the disappointments of her relationship, she committed to learning to love fully the man she was involved with. She did this rather than secretly withholding, because there was part of her that believed that "he really wasn't the one." She did this rather than rationalizing that she he wasn't giving her what she most wanted, so she shouldn't have to give to him.

Soon after that a letter came from David. This was the boy she had fallen in love with when she was 17, the man she had always loved the best, but never knew how to create a good relationship with, and from whom she hadn't heard a word in many years. He had traced her through old friends and was writing to reconnect, because he was now divorced and had never stopped thinking about her. In her newly established integrity of giving her best to work, to love, to life, she felt deserving of love and happiness in a way she never had before. She could also feel the ability in her to sustain this new rela- tionship—through the bad times and the good. All that meant it was easy to say "yes" when she and David decided to get married six months later. They have now been married for almost 20 years, and Joanna is grateful every day for the spiritual practice of giving her best—no matter what.

Questions for Meditation and Journal Work

1. Thinking back over the last few days, can you recollect instances where you had a choice to hold yourself back or to give? Did you hold back because of old grudges, resentments, or arrogant pride? Or did you sponta- neously give of yourself as much as the opportuni- ty provided?

2. Are you willing to courageously give of yourself even when you are not assured of receiving anything in return? Or do you hold yourself back, insisting that you must know that you will indeed receive before you final- ly do give of yourself?

3. Could there be a balance to life where you will be able to receive life's abundance to the extent that you generously squander your inner riches (love, integrity, dedication, etc.) into life? Could it be that giving and receiving are one and the same

flow, and that one cannot manifest without the other? If you accept this possibility, what parts of you may be resisting or blocking this understanding?

4. Consider that true giving is an act of love, not a display intended to generate the admiration of others. Could the difficulties associated with receiving your sought-after fulfillment, at least in part, be attributed to your unwillingness to truly give of yourself? If so, how?

5. Do you refuse to give to yourself by suppressing your feelings, by blocking your intuition, and/or by preventing other aspects of your inner being from spontaneously coming forward? If so, how?

Believing Life Will Provide What's Needed

"Am I taking this momentary limitation as something I can use to defeat a beautiful moment, or am I willing to have the faith that all limitations are only a reflection of the limitation of my mind and my concept? As you widen your own concept, these limitations will disappear. The next question you can ask yourself is: 'Do I have enough faith in what I am doing that I can do it in the spirit of love and the knowledge that all of my material needs will be filled, even if there is, at this moment, some economic compromise necessary?'"

(Additional Material 3)

Affirmation

I acknowledge that my will does not need to be done in order for me to be happy. I accept my current situation as a necessary stepping stone on the path toward my sought-after fulfillment.

Jimmy's Story

While Jimmy was toiling at his job one day, he realized he didn't want to spend the rest of his life working for other people. He felt he was an entrepreneur at heart. What he needed, however, was an idea for a business he could start. He looked around and realized that one division of the company where he worked was underutilized. He sensed he could start his own business by actualizing the potential of that neglected part of the business! With idea and plans in hand, he obtained financing from a friend and then marched into the jungle of the New York City real estate market to find office space. He viewed many spaces, but one dazzled him. It was a loft, large, airy, and bright. He had always dreamt of having a loft! Visions of conducting a successful business in this beautiful space filled his mind. He was falling in love with the space. But, of course, it was expensive. Could his business, yet to be born, afford this high rent? He wondered if he should risk a high rent and take the space he loved? Or, should he be more prudent and conservative and take a much smaller, less interesting, and cheaper space? His mind spun around between these two alternatives. Finally, quite confused, he asked God for guidance. He sat down with his journal and requested help. What came through during that session was: "A baby needs a crib, not a king-sized bed!" The logic of that simple statement clarified what he needed to do. With much disappointment, but less anxiety, he said "good-bye" to the loft and secured a lease on a less expensive office. Within a short time of launching his new venture, the then-thriving economy stumbled into a recession. Many businesses failed, and Jimmy's accountant, doubting the soundness of the business, suggested that Jimmy close it as well. Carried by his vision of being a successful entrepreneur, Jimmy persevered and survived the recession. The business is now over 22 years old and employs 10 full-time people. It has branched into related ventures and has done well. Had Jimmy allowed his fascination with the beautiful loft space lead him, his firm probably would not in business today. Thanks to his guidance, as well as his willingness to ask and then listen, Jimmy has made his business, through sound judgment and hard work, a success.

Questions for Meditation and Journal Work

1. Are the "sacrifices" you currently make really damaging or jeopardizing you? Or are they instead a challenge to your idealized self-image (who you imagine or wish yourself to be)?

2. When it comes to your sought-after fulfillment, do you fear you will not get what you need? If so, could this fear be a prohibition standing in the way of experiencing the sought-after fulfillment? What would need to happen for you instead to hold the manifestation of this fulfillment simply as a creative expression of your God-connected self?

3. If a child is not yet grown, and it is angry, impatient, and judgmental about not yet being grown, is this not wasted energy and a denial of the growth process? If an adult is not yet where he or she wants to be and is angry, impatient, and judgmental, is this not a waste of energy? Is it not a denial of the beauty of, and the nature of the growth process? If you accept this idea, find the places in you where you refuse to accept the current circumstances of your life.

4. Are you willing to view your current circumstances as appropriate given your current state of spiritual development, and also an accurate reflection of this same state of development? Can you imagine how these circumstances would change as you change yourself?

5. Consider that following the will of God will not deprive you. Are you willing to consider that by increasingly surrendering to God, you will progressively open to abundance?

Envisioning an Unimpeded Life

"Do an exercise in trust in which you open yourself to the possibility that the universe will yield whatever you need. Experiment for the moment with the thought: 'How would it be if I were to trust the universe? If in this particular situation I gave up the fear that comes from my distrust, and therefore from pride and self-will?' Allow your central core to fill you with an inkling of a state in which you can react without self-will, pride, and fear."   (Pathwork Guide Lecture 203)

Affirmation

I feel the supportive nature of life, where nothing needs to be feared, where I am being guided to the work I must do in order to materialize a life of fulfillment.

Michelle's Story

It had been two years since Michelle had gone through a painful divorce, and her ex-husband was madly in love with another woman. She felt unlovable because she was not in a passionate and deep relationship with a man. She had gone through several boyfriends in an effort not to be alone, in order not to feel the emptiness inside herself. But none of these men were the one she felt she was meant to be with. In her desperation to be in relationship, she was too quick to say yes to men who just happened to come into her life. Her pride wanted her to look good, to be in a relationship with an attractive man, so that she would feel like she was a desirable woman. Her fear spoke to her as self-doubts, making her worry that she was not in fact lovable. Her self-will said that she had to be in such a relationship, that she was nobody without a man. She was surprised to see these tightly held attitudes and beliefs inside herself, and she then realized they were the reasons she had not been able to bring love and happiness into her life. Through individual counseling sessions with a spiritual teacher, she did more deep work to understand and accept her pride, her self-will, and her fear. This allowed her to relax into a new state, where she trusted the universe, where she could allow life to give to her what she deserved. At this same time she realized that her happiness was not generated by external factors, but that she needed to take responsibility for generating her own happiness. She decided to put God's will above her own. In the process of releasing her desperation, she could feel the joy and fullness already present in her life. She appreciated that she had much to be thankful for, including a great son, a good job, a number of close friends, and a wonderful community. She felt how fulfilling her life was even though she still longed for relationship. About three months later a man who was not only excited to be with her, but who also saw and appreciated her on many levels, came into her life. In this relationship, she experienced a deeper love, joy, and pleasure than she had ever imagined possible.

Questions for Meditation and Journal Work

1. Are you waiting for good feelings to be created by outside circumstances or by other people? Or are you generating your own good feelings, self-esteem, and self-love?

2. Can you envision yourself in a state where your sought-after fulfillment is manifested, where you are not forcefully willing this manifestation? Can you envision this scene in a way where you are neither directed by your self-will nor exploited by others, where you assert yourself but also let go and give in to the truth?

3. Have you been trying to do everything to manifest your sought-after goal? Could you instead act like a gardener, establishing the right conditions for seeds to grow, and trusting that nature (or God) will do the rest? Could establishing the right conditions in this case involve clearing away your internal blocks?

4. If you don't get exactly what you want, delivered the way you want it, right now, does this feel like you have lost? Could you still win if you got something else instead, perhaps something that was better than your originally sought-after fulfillment?

5. Imagine that the universal forces (God) flow through you in an unimpeded way, that every breath is a prayer, and that every action you take is an expression of love, truth, purposefulness, and creativity. When it comes to your life, what might be getting in the way of living like this?

Understanding Wishful Daydreaming

"Let us be very clear about the difference between wishful thinking and the realism and courage of positive belief. . . . Wishful thinking is spinning dreams of fulfillment without any price having been paid: without any change of personality, of attitude, of approach to thinking, of feeling, of acting, of being. You spin the dream that this or that desirable fulfillment will come your way, magically and gratuitously. But there is no investment of yourself into life, into the process of creation, into contributing to the evolutionary process by the commitment to your own purification process. It is all a passive dreaming in which you hope against hope that something will happen to you that is desirable and that does not require you to remove the very block that prevents this desirable event or state. The less you invest into yourself that which could make all these desirable events or states a reality, the less can you believe in the actual manifestation of these fulfillments, the more justified the superstition of pessimism, the less desirable your life becomes, the more you wish to escape from it . . . this consumes a lot of creative energy that could be invested into real living and fulfillment." (Pathwork Guide Lecture 236)

Affirmation

I accept the struggle of life, and I commit to keep taking constructive steps to manifest my desired goals.

Dan's Story

Dan had just split up with his girlfriend of eight years, Wendy. Wendy was very bitter about his departure and had many choice but unprintable words to describe his personality. Up until recently, for many years they had lived together in a house and shared the expenses. Dan had also taken 10 months off from his job as a construction contractor to completely remodel the house. In return for his effort, Wendy had verbally promised to give Dan a portion of the equity in the house. The house was legally in her name, and she intended to continue to live there. After the breakup, she not only refused to put their agreement in writing, but she also refused to get a second mortgage or home equity loan so that Dan could get his money out. Dan was angry that Wendy was not living up to her word and that he wasn't going to get his money anytime soon. Coincidental to his leaving Wendy, Dan had reentered school to become a business coach. Going to school instead of working as much as he had in the past on construction jobs further eroded his spending power. Then his old truck had a major breakdown and it really wasn't worth fixing. Dan desperately needed a truck so he could bring in food and rent money while he continued his studies. In a conversation with his father, Dan mentioned that he needed to buy a used truck, but he didn't mention the fact that he didn't have enough money to buy one.

Dan was tense because he didn't know how he was going to get the money without dropping out of school for a while. Dan had always worked hard for everything—all that he had accumulated seemed to be the result of sweat and hard labor. He began to drift into fantasy, imaging the ways the universe would provide a new truck and some extra cash. He then realized this was wishful thinking and daydreaming. Contrary to how he would have approached this matter in the past, Dan affirmed to himself that he would do whatever it took, and he felt confident that he was soon going to get a new truck. A few days later, Dan saw his family for Christmas. Dan was delighted and amazed at the synchronicity of it all when his father announced his intention to buy a new car for each of his now-grown children. Because the economy was going through a down phase, the auto dealers were offering zero percent financing, and Dan's father couldn't resist a good deal like that. Dan's father also had a lot of money that was likely to have gone to the government with the estate tax, money that he would rather give to his children. So Dan was reminded of the power of his intention, of his faith that it would work out, and of a larger meaning to life beyond what he could see in front of him. He began to appreciate that maybe life wasn't so hard after all, that maybe things could come to him more naturally if he were to expect the best but also be willing to do whatever it takes.

Questions for Meditation and Journal Work

1. Do you spend a significant part of your time brooding, worrying, or going back over pessimistic and negative thoughts? Would this time be better used shifting your internal state as well as taking specific actions to create the future you desire?

2. Are your daydreams a way to prop up your ego or to make you feel better about yourself? Are they motivated by revenge, impressing others, or other intentions that compensate for past hurts or perceived personal deficiencies?

3. Do your daydreams contain scenarios where your sought-after fulfillment is gratuitously given to you, where you don't have to work for it? Are you willing to adopt a more self-responsible attitude?

4. Do you prefer to live in your daydreams because the present situation seems too much for you? If so, what is it about the fantasy world that seems so much more desirable than the wonder of life in this moment?

5. What is getting in the way of you creating a relaxed inner state, an expectant, flexible, life affirming, positive, and inclusive attitude regarding the fulfillment you desire? How do you defeat the abundance that wants to flow into your life with an angry, exclusive, negative, tense, impatient, and stubborn attitude?

Day 11

Getting Clear about Your Intentions

"Again, with money it is as with all other things. The principle is the same. When money is used as a means to an end, not a goal in itself, then the integration is right. When a person consciously determines not to be bound to matter by money but to use it like all other gifts of God, such as health or any talent, in a spirit of gratefulness, to use the freedom from worries that money can provide to intensify his or her spiritual development, then the integration is just right."
(Pathwork Guide Lecture 8)

Affirmation

I see how my desired fulfillment is good and right for everyone concerned, how it empowers me to make additional contributions to life, and how it advances the manifestation of God's will for my life.

Gwen's Story

Gwen had been a self-supporting adult student for several years and had next to no disposable income. Yet she loved music, loved to make music, and viewed it as an offering to God. She had learned to play the piano as a child and was a talented musician, but her circumstances in the middle of a large city didn't provide access to a piano. She worked on her intentions regarding having a piano, examining them from many different angles. She deeply prayed for clarity of purpose, for a unified intention consistent with God's will, to manifest a piano in her life. She then let it go, that is to say that however God decided to manifest a piano (or not) was acceptable to her. Separately, in exchange for tuition in one of the two schools she was attending, she worked as a secretary, handling applications from students and interviewing those students who looked like good candidates for the school. Instead of doing the traditional interview on the school premises, one applicant took a more informal approach, asking her out for coffee. Over coffee they talked about a number of topics that were not school related, including the fact that this applicant had just bought a new piano. He also had a high-quality older piano and he asked Gwen whether she knew of anybody who might want it. She piped up that she loved playing the piano and that she would be delighted to take it off his hands. That very afternoon, he had movers relocate the piano to her apartment, and for the next ten years, until she moved across the country, she enjoyed playing this marvelous instrument.

Questions for Meditation and Journal Work

1. Make a list of all the intentions behind your desire for a particular type of abundance. Then review this list and ask yourself some questions. For example, do you believe this type of abundance will help you obtain the love and respect of others? Do you seek revenge, or are you intent on proving a point? Are you attempting to get something you did not have as a child? Are your reasons consistent with the Pathwork Guide quote at beginning of this chapter?

2. Is the fulfillment you seek motivated by being values (love, truth, serving God, personal growth, etc.)? Or is it motivated by appearance values (covering the unpleasant truth, impressing others, being better than others, etc.)? Or perhaps by some mix of the two?

3. How is the unfulfilled longing in your life a reflection of something within yourself that you have not adequately focused on, that you have not yet brought out into the light to be healed?

4. Make a list of every party who may be affected if your sought-after abundance were to be manifested. Is the abundance you desire truly good and right for all parties concerned? Do you clearly see that there is nothing destructive about the sought-after fulfillment? If so, can you open to the possibility of being free from reservations about creating it in your life? If you still feel as though there is something destructive about your fulfillment, ask yourself whether this destruction serves a higher good (for example because it opens the way for something much better to follow).

5. Is the way you hold the sought-after abundance characterized by impatience, inflexibility, judgment, and insistence? If so, it may be the intention of the limited ego within you.

However, if your desired abundance is characterized by patience, flexibility, openness, and acceptance, then the intention comes from a deeper place, a place consistent with the will of God. Abundance with the latter is readily manifested, while abundance with the former is not. If your own fulfillment is the intention of your ego, consider how you might change your intention to make it consistent with the will of God.

Creating an Open Energy System

"The attitude characteristic of an open energy system would be something like this: 'I would love you to love me. You seem to be the person I would like to share myself with and to whom I would like to give all of myself. If you are that person, I know that you must come to me in freedom, out of your own volition. Even if my forcing could affect you, I would not want it this way. I trust the universe to give me what is my fair due. If you do not wish this freely, I can let you go from deep within and wait in faith that the person who will appreciate and freely want what I have to give will come to me.' This attitude reflects an open energy system and is compatible with the abundance available. Abundance constantly floats around you, but your clogged energy system erects a wall that closes you off from the ever-present abundance. Of course, the same principle applies to all other kinds of relationships: to wanting a specific job, wanting friends, wanting people who will buy what you have to sell, who will receive what you have to give, or who give you what you look for."

(Pathwork Guide Lecture 213)

Affirmation

In humility, strength, truth, and confidence, I affirm my openness to receiving what the universe wants to give me. I see that I don't need to force other people to do anything or to be any particular way.

Mira's Story

Mira had been experiencing difficulty, frustration, and a sense of failure in her intimate partnerships over the last

20 years. Her two long-term relationships gave her ample opportunity to grow spiritually, yet they both fell short of the soul connection she deeply desired. After leaving her lover of four years, Mira entered a period of meditation, prayer, and introspection. During this period she realized that she continued her family legacy of disappointment and defeat in her relationships with men. Her parents were frustrated in marriage. Both of them felt as if they were trapped by circumstances and forced to be with someone other than the one they genuinely desired. This feeling came about because Mira's mother had gotten pregnant and her parents had rushed into marriage a few months before she was born. Like them, Mira expected to be frustrated and unfulfilled in relationship. Mira had also believed that men held the key to deep soul contact and merging for her. This belief caused her to be a predator who hunted down love and fulfillment from men. Since the power to unleash and unlock these deep states was given to men, Mira became clingy, anxious, and dependent because she never knew whether her lover would answer her longing. Through painful interactions with her most recent lover, solitude, and inner guidance, she then discovered that the key to her deepest fulfillment was in her own heart. At that point, she began a new journey of self-love, compassion, and healing. As Mira let go of her illusory need to get love from outside herself, she relaxed into the abundant and loving core of her own being. She then let herself simultaneously be love, the lover, and "the beloved" (an intimate manifestation of God).

Questions for Mediation and Journal Work

1. Consider how the feeling behind "you must love me" is not really love at all. Consider how this forcing current does not allow another person to have freedom or free choice. Have you been saying "you must give it to me" in some area of your life? If so, how have you been saying this?

2. A closed energy system is characterized by forcefulness, domination, demands, jealous behavior, and possessiveness. Feelings like this, whether or not they are accompanied by overt behavior, are a response to a negative expectation about life. Do you ever feel or act like this? Probe below the surface and see if you can come up with evidence and examples.

3. Could it be that the abundance life wants to give you is inaccessible because you tightly hold onto a particular way it should be, because you force life to give you this particular type of abundance?

4. Close your eyes and visualize yourself moving into a space of humility, where you stop blaming the universe for not giving you what you want, where you instead search for the distortions that prevent your sought-after abundance from being manifested. How does this feel?

5. Consider that your present life's circumstances fairly and accurately reflect your current state of consciousness. To facilitate changes in these circumstances, how might you change your current state of consciousness?

Transitioning from a "No-Current" to a "Yes-Current"

"I want this goal with all my heart. I have nothing to fear from it."Meditating on why there is nothing to fear, why the old fear was false, and why the new accepting attitude to the life experience, according to the right concept, is entirely safe, is the final step in moving from a No-Current to a Yes-Current." (Pathwork Guide Lecture 125)

Affirmation

I now bring those parts of me that say "no" forward into consciousness, with the intention of reaching inner alignment and accessing my dormant potentials.

Colette's Story

A few years ago, Colette's oldest brother, Dennis, had reached the final stages of infection with the AIDS virus. As a result, he needed full-time care. Dennis neither had the resources nor the tolerance for "strangers" to take care of him. At the same time, nobody in the family had the means, the time, or the inclination to take care of him. For Colette this was a special hardship, because she ran her own small business, which needed a lot of attention. Colette called her siblings and Dennis's kids, all of whom had some peeve about Dennis. (He was a difficult guy even for those who liked him.) It became clear that

Colette was on her own, at least for the moment. In a painful and revealing conversation with one sibling, Colette asked, "Regardless of what you feel about him, you have a dying brother. Does that not move you?!!" At that moment a very remarkable thing happened to Colette. She realized at a very deep level and in that instant that she had made a complete and unreserved commitment to see Dennis to his last breath. She felt that her attention on a deep level was focused very intensely and lovingly on Dennis, that she was going to give him whatever he needed. Within three days, Colette had changed every contract her small business had. She rearranged her work so that all the contracts were based in the same city where she and Dennis lived (so travel was not necessary); involved writing, which she could do anywhere and anytime; or was deferred with an advance on fees. Colette then had more than she could hope for materially, and this allowed her to give her brother real help at every level. Colette deeply enjoyed the intimacy of those last months, despite the inevitability of Dennis's death. During that period, he made peace with the entire family and with his life. He became friends with God again. His last words to his closest friend were: "I die surrounded by love."

Questions for Meditation and Journal Work

1. Is the conscious yes-current regarding your desired fulfillment urgent and frantic? Consider the possibility that these feelings are a tip-off that there are one or more no-currents that are unconscious. Consider the possibility that these two currents pull your personality in two directions simultaneously, and thus create tension.

2. Is there a part of yourself that is saying "no" to a commitment you have made, or are thinking of making? Could your dissatisfaction about and trouble with this commitment be attributable to this "no"? How could this be happening?

3. When you discover a subtle but distinct "no" to a fulfillment you desire, can you accept it? Can you refrain from arguing it away, rationally explaining it, denying it, suppressing it, or being impatient with yourself? Can you just let it be while you work on it?

4. Is there part of you that believes that if you bring up your "no" to a cherished fulfillment, it will be permanent, final, and static? Consider that this "no" is permanent, final, and static only to the extent that you cling to it and allow yourself to be controlled by it.

5. Have you ever truly committed to something, such that you had a one-pointed focus and every part of you was aligned with that goal? If so, can you apply the way you approached that commitment to the abundance you now seek?

Understanding Your Idealized Self-Image

"You will know exactly when you have weakened your idealized self by fully understanding its function, its causes, and its effects. Then you will gain the freedom of giving yourself to life because you no longer have to hide something from yourself and others. You will be able to squander yourself into life, not in an unhealthy, unreasonable way, but healthily as nature squanders herself. Then, and only then, will you know the beauty of living."

(Pathwork Guide Lecture 83)

Affirmation

*I have no need to pretend that I am anything
or anyone other than my true self.*

Anne's Story

Anne had been struggling for several years in a marriage that wasn't working. Part of the reason she hung in there was her son, who was then 10 years old. She knew in her gut that there were major problems with the marriage, but she kept trying to twist herself into a shape that would make the marriage work. She had developed a pattern where she would compromise herself in order to provide what she thought other people wanted. She then began to examine who she thought she had to be for other people, her idealized self-image, and how dif-

ferent this was from who she really was. Soon thereafter
she began to present her real needs, her feelings, her
thoughts, and her true essence to her husband. A crisis
followed because she was no longer the woman he
wanted her to be. After a while she clearly saw that her
husband didn't want the real version of herself; he wanted who she had previously been presenting to the world.
She then understood she had moved into a more rapid
growth phase in her spiritual evolution, and he wasn't
going to support it. At that point Anne understood that
to stay with him would have been living a lie; it would
have been against spiritual truth. She saw the only way
that she could bring pleasure and abundance into her
life was to act in accordance with this knowing. Anne
knew that in taking care of herself, her son would get
what he needed. She also knew that she had to let go of
a structure that no longer worked and began challenging
her old idealized self-image. She went on to get a
divorce and is now elated to be in love with a man who
not only supports her in showing the world who
she really is, but who also sees the beauty in her real self.

Questions for Meditation and Journal Work

1. Do you act falsely or inauthentically to get love or protection from other people? If so, how? And if you know how, are these strategies really working?

2. Are you in touch with the deeply hidden fear that says your world will come to an end if you do not live up to the dictates of your idealized self-image? Is this fear grounded in truth?

3. Can you accept yourself as you are now, in spite of the fact that you don't meet the exaggerated demands and stringent standards of your idealized self-image?

4. Are you willing to consider that the standards and dictates of your idealized self-image can never be attained? Are you willing to admit the impossibility of living up to these perfectionistic requirements? Are you ready to stop whipping yourself for failing to meet the demands of your idealized self-image?

5. As long as you aspire to be your idealized self-image, won't you be permeated with the guilt of being something you are not? And how can you have self-confidence if this guilt undermines you, repeatedly saying that you are a fraud?

Releasing Perfectionism

"The humility of giving up perfectionism, the honesty to pay the price for developing slowly into a more genuinely perfect being are indispensable prerequisites which are, in fact, aspects of perfection already. It may seem paradoxical: by accepting humbly your limitations, your imperfect state, and looking at it creatively, constructively, and specifically, so as to understand and make connections, is already a manifestation of the Divinity within you."

(Pathwork Guide Lecture 234)

Affirmation

The more I accept the imperfection of my life, my situation, and my consciousness, the more I experience both joy and happiness.

Gordon's Story

Gordon had been a bachelor for 41 years. He was in and out of lots of relationships, but always looking for "Miss Right." He even had a list of the 10 most important qualities a woman should have, and he thought a woman had to have at least eight of these to be "the one." Then he met an interesting woman, and what went through his mind was, "Here is a woman I could be friends with." To his surprise he found that he was very excited by this meeting, and for the next few days he just couldn't get this woman out of his mind. He called her and found out that she too had been thinking a great deal about him.

So they started dating, in spite of the fact that she didn't appear to meet his criteria. He found himself falling in love with her, with all the stomach flutters and swells of exuberance. After six months, they hit a snag in the relationship where a lot of issues came up. These included jealousy, security, communication, and other problems. At that point they decided to get help, so they went to a relationship seminar together. After that, they diligently and enthusiastically worked on exposing their fears to each other, on identifying the erroneous images they had about relationship, and on overcoming the blocks to intimacy they both harbored. Although they still argued occasionally, they adopted an intention to work things out, a mutual commitment to discover the other person, and a willingness not to run away. Soon thereafter they moved in together. Things were fine for two years, at which point she told him she wanted to get married. Gordon was terrified and all the same questions about "Miss Right" came up again. He worried whether she was the one he really wanted, and he wondered if he was willing to give up his ideas about the perfect woman. During the course of three sessions with his spiritual teacher, Gordon imagined himself in several future scenarios. What would it be like to say "yes" to her? What would it be like to say "no" to her and risk losing the relationship? What would it be like to admit, on a deeper level, how much he really loved her? Thanks to these sessions, he had a breakthrough and appreciated how his perfectionism was holding him back. He rushed home and invited her to go on a mountain hike with him to a secluded spot. When they got to the special spot, with heart pounding fiercely, he dropped to his knees and asked her to marry him. The wedding was the happiest day of Gordon's life. His joy knew no bounds, and he thought his face would split apart from smiling so wide. Now that he has been happily married five years, he thinks that getting married was the best thing he ever did. Together they have built a solid base of love, trust, commitment, acceptance, and understanding. Every once in a while she will tell Gordon something that she has never told him before, and he will see a new facet of this marvelous being—his wife.

Questions for Meditation and Journal Work

1. Do you see how your claim for perfection is in opposition to truth? Do you see how this means that your claim for perfection can never be reflected by reality?

2. Are there aspects of your personality in which you make believe you are perfect? Does this pretense amount to cheating life in the sense that you don't want to do the work to evolve yourself, that you want the result without having paid the price?

3. Are you willing to accept that you are a Divine creation and that you are here on earth to evolve the imperfect parts of yourself? Wouldn't an acceptance of these imperfections foster your spiritual growth?

4. What are your motives for striving for perfection? Do you want to be better than others? Do you want to hide your own feelings of worthlessness? Or do you seek to come closer to God by honestly and patiently working on your imperfections?

5. Can you feel how your perfectionism is isolating and unloving? Can you see how you are focused on appearing a certain way, rather than focused on the true needs of yourself and others?

Overcoming Negative Beliefs

"There is nothing that you cannot realize. There is nothing you cannot experience if you truly give yourself to it, if you remove the anchor that prevents you from this new flowing expansion, and if you allow the involuntary processes with their limitless possibilities to carry you and bring you to ever new shores of fulfillment. This courageous faith in the best of your own inner spirit must be asserted. The courage lies in bridging the gap between assertion of the faith and the realization—until it bears fruit. The temptation to lean on the old superstitious negative beliefs comes from there not being a waiting period, no uncertainty, no growing phase. As you speak the negative belief, so it occurs. You have the questionable certainty of immediate results that you are so keen on." (Pathwork Guide Lecture 236)

Affirmation

I challenge each of my negative beliefs, and also give myself some time to become accustomed to a new and more positive attitude toward life.

Erica's Story

Erica has always been an independent spirit. From the time she was very young, reports her mother, she was known for indignantly saying "I help MYSELF!" whenever she was offered assistance. To Erica, an offer of help implied that she was incapable or inadequate. As the oldest of three children, her tendency toward independence was welcomed by her busy mother and not seen as anything but positive. Additionally, Erica was quite competent in many areas and was seeming to prosper. What no one noticed, however, were the stresses and demands she was heaping on herself. After all, she had to do everything all by herself! The pressures grew and the stress affected her physical and emotional health.

By the time she was a high school sophomore, she was often ill, and occasionally she was depressed with suicidal thoughts. There were times she was afraid her head would just explode. College presented more of the same stresses. When she did ask for help, the professors were demeaning, further strengthening her image that she had to do it herself or be diminished. In her 30s, after some personal growth and spiritual work, Erica opened to other possibilities. She began to realize that her beliefs about life shaped the course of her life. And then, one great day, when she was up against the wall and ready to scream, it dawned on her that she can ask for help and still be respected, strong, and loved. She understood that she didn't have to wait until it is almost too late. She saw how it is not shameful to ask for help. It is, instead, realistic and gives other people an opportunity to do something they might feel good doing. Following this "Ah-Ha!" experience, it has been much easier for Erica to ask for help. She was willing to be vulnerable, to risk being refused, and even to feel some residual feelings of embarrassment at times. It took time to change her old habits of self-reliance, but she now remembers to ask when she needs help, and sometimes even before she needs help. On occasion, she even asks for help just for the fun and contact, even though she could have managed on her own. She has realized that some of the most fulfilling moments in her life have been working on group projects with others toward a common goal. She savors these times of cooperation and camaraderie. As an extension of this, Erica often asks for help from the spiritual world. She routinely receives this help for requests from the mundane (like locating parking spaces) to the ephemeral (like helping someone in another part of the world heal themselves). She is delighted with the response she has received from the unmanifest consciousness that surrounds us all and reminds us that we are all connected and that, indeed, there is an abundance of help available for all!

Questions for Meditation and Journal Work

1. What major beliefs do you have about the ways your desired fulfillment must be manifested? Are you open to having them be untrue?

2. Are you willing to take personal responsibility for your own spiritual growth, but at the same time willing to admit that you cannot do it alone? Are you genuinely open to receiving assistance not only from other people, but also from God?

3. Is there part of you that thinks your life will never change, that all you can expect is unhappiness, that nothing good is going to come to you? How might this expectation create exactly that in your life experience?

4. Are you willing to assert your belief in a positive experience of life? Without any assurance of success, can you have faith that a genuinely good outcome is possible?

5. Deep down inside you, is there a part of you that thinks that if you believe in the positive, you will be disappointed? Does this part of you think that by believing in the positive, you may chase it away, or that you may in some manner jinx yourself?

Dealing with Impatience

"Everything in the universe moves in this constant ebb and flow. It is the pulsing movement of life. Expansion-contraction. Each phase brings another aspect of reality to experience for consciousness. . . . I show you that both ends of the spectrum can be positive, good, desirable, rather than one being good, the other being bad. So it is with your case. If you were not so insecure, you would enjoy the phases of the ebb, of contraction in a spirit of giving yourself a rest. But what is this insecurity? It is nothing more or less than lack of faith and understanding. The more you flow with the moment, the ebb periods will only serve to gather your strength and to claim your faith in life's abundance, preparing you for the next phase of expansion, of fullness, of activity." (Pathwork Guide Lecture 254)

Affirmation

If I have not yet fully manifested my sought-after fulfillment, there must still be some work I need to do to clear the way.

Amy's Story

Amy was the rental manager for a large healing center used by many different spiritual groups. During the five years she had worked there, rental income had increased 400 percent. Amy ran only a single ad in a big-city quarterly journal. She sometimes got a lot of pressure from her peers to expand her advertising, but she knew deep within what was causing the increase in business. First was the simple act of prayer—asking God to send rentals to fill specific dates on the center's calendar. She had been skeptical herself in the beginning, but prayer worked so consistently that she focused on that as her primary "advertising medium." Often Amy would sit at her desk gazing at an empty spot on the calendar and say, "God, we need a rental for that date." Soon thereafter, a phone call would come, asking for precisely that date.

Next, she had to find any place in her or the rest of the staff where a "no" to abundance existed. She held a staff meeting where she had the staff members voice their longings. It was touching how often the longing of staff members was to enrich people's experience at the center. Then Amy had them voice their "no." Increasing business meant more work, more problems, more complexity at the center. Then, while still acknowledging their resistance, they all affirmed their longing and prayed together. In the next week the phone rang with three new rentals. A year later Amy tried this again with the center's board of directors. The phones rang with five more rentals the next day. Despite some people accusing Amy of "magical thinking," she knew this was true mutuality between her and Spirit. God's abundance is that easy to achieve when we uncover and face our resistance to it.

Amy often said that God gave you either what you wanted or what you needed. The trick is to stay open to every apparent absence of abundance and to be curious about the meaning of it. One year she had two vacant weekends in May, and no matter how much she prayed, she was frustrated because no rentals appeared for those two weekends. Then in January of that same year there were major snowstorms on two consecutive weekends, forc-

ing the center to cancel its most important classes. Once
the snow was cleared, Amy looked at the schedule to
find when these two classes could be rescheduled. She
was both amazed and delighted when she realized that
the only two weekends available were the two she had
prayed so hard to fill. These two classes were fundamental to the center's mission, and it would have been very
costly if they had to be canceled. So despite Amy's
prayers for more rentals, God was watching out for them
and knew what they needed.

Questions for Meditation and Journal Work

1. Consider that impatience would not exist if you were
certain about a specific result. What specifically do you
have doubts about, and are these doubts grounded and
in truth?

2. Have you made some erroneous conclusions about
time? Is the inner child inside you causing you to rush
ahead, causing you to think that you absolutely must
have your desired fulfillment immediately?

3. Deep down inside yourself, do you believe that to be
happy, you must have what you want, exactly the way
that you want it, right now? Could this demanding attitude, this lack of flexibility, actually impede the manifestation of happiness in your life?

4. Can you see how everything has a purpose, and that
the difficulties you now experience may actually be necessary for your eventual fulfillment? Are you willing to
ask God for assistance so that you can understand the
reasons for the difficulties you are now experiencing?

5. Just as the sea has tides with an ebb and a flow, so you have your own unique inner rhythms. Ask God to help you feel these inner rhythms. Are you living your life in harmony with these rhythms?

Cultivating Receptivity to God's Will

"Whatever I already am, I want to devote to life. I deliberately want life to make use of the best of what I have and who I am. I may not be sure at this moment in what way this could happen, and even if I have ideas, I will allow for the greater intelligence and wisdom deep within me to guide me. I will let life itself decide how a fruitful interchange can take place between it and me. For whatever I give to life, I have received from it, and I wish to return it to the great cosmic pool to bring more benefit to others. This, in turn, must inevitably enrich my own life to the exact measure that I willingly give to life; for truly life and I are one. When I withhold from life, I withhold from myself. When I withhold from others, I withhold from myself. Whatever I already am, I want to let flow into life. And whatever more in me can be utilized, still waiting to be brought to fruition, I request, I decide, and I desire that it be put to constructive use, so as to enrich the atmosphere around me." (Pathwork Guide Lecture 138)

Affirmation

I now give myself wholeheartedly to life and to God. I overcome my inertia, and with the best of intentions, I do, I act, and I risk, so that I can receive all of what the universe wishes to give me.

Monica's Story

Monica and Jim were monogamous lovers for 17 years. One day she called a friend of hers, a woman who was in her women's group. Instead of her friend Fran, she reached Fran's daughter Andrea. Monica asked to speak to Fran, and Andrea told her that Fran wasn't there, that Fran was out with Jim. Just an hour or so earlier, Jim had called Monica to tell her that he couldn't see her that day because he had a lot of personal shopping to do. At that moment Monica understood what was happening, that Jim was cheating on her and lying about it. She felt like she was going to throw up and pass out. She sat down on her couch after the telephone call in an effort to get grounded. At that moment she had what she calls a "Divine intervention." She heard a voice ask: "What do you want to give yourself now?" She surrendered to the voice and asked: "What are my choices?" She first heard the obvious choice, which was to feel betrayed, wronged, abandoned, and unlovable. She decided she didn't deserve that, because she hadn't done anything—Jim was the one who cheated on her. She asked herself: "What is the other choice?" At that point she had a vision of her choices: to go swimming in a sewage pond (the first option) or in a beautiful healing lake. She chose the healing lake, and then her heart opened to herself, she saw that she was the source of her own happiness, and she was deeply moved by that. She saw that whatever her lover did could not really take away from her. This brought her to a state of grace. The next day people at work and around town remarked that she was glowing, and they wanted to give her a hug. The state of grace remained even though she remembered how she could have chosen to be a very different way that day.

Questions for Meditation and Journal Work

1. Think back over your life and see if you can remember short periods of time when you had an experience of life that was not far different from the experience defined in the quote at the beginning of this chapter. If you can remember no such times, see whether there isn't some deep inner knowing inside of you that remembers an experience like this. Can you recapture the feeling of this experience, even if only for a brief moment?

2. Consider that your experience is constantly being created as a result of your consciousness, attitudes, thoughts, and beliefs. How could your experience shift if you adopted the position described in the quote at the beginning of this chapter?

3. Consider that you are already all that you could ever wish to be. Consider that you already possess the states of consciousness you wish to experience. Consider that your deep spiritual work releases that same Divine part of you that is now covered over by misconceptions, errors, and so forth. Does this perspective change the way you look at yourself?

4. Rather than being passive and receiving whatever comes your way, consider that you need significant activity and willpower to fulfill God's will. Specifically, how might both significant activity and willpower be needed for you to evolve yourself in a manner consistent with God's will?

5. Consider that when you have a deep and abiding commitment to give the best of yourself to life, and when all of your motives are clear, then you will experience

that your heart's desire is also God's will. How might this change the way you look at your sought-after fulfillment?

Viewing Problems and Difficulties as Gifts

"Show me, Father, the real reasons for my difficulties so that I can solve them. Do not ask that this difficulty be simply taken away. That would be the wrong and immature way of asking."   (Pathwork Guide Lecture 17)

Affirmation

I open to the possibility that it is God's will that I become mature, independent, and self-responsible. I hold the difficulties I experience as gifts from the world of Spirit intended to support my movement in this direction.

Carrie's Story

Carrie came from a middle-class family, but her father had barely survived the Great Depression, and like many folks from that time, was so deeply afraid that he could never let himself or his children enjoy feeling safe or abundant financially. Carrie had the education and training to earn a good living, but in her mid-30s found herself increasingly making choices that resulted in living in poverty. As her mother said, she was living in "hovels" and with just enough money to keep going. As a client in therapy for many years and then additional years as a practitioner of a spiritual path that examined consciousness in all things, she found many roots to this

pattern. One by one she gave up using her poor circumstances to punish herself and others: as spite toward her
parents for their failings, as illusory superiority against
those who were more abundant and therefore "too
materialistic," as a defense against not being as successful as others thought she would be, and so forth. As a
result of this spiritual work, many things in her outer life
changed: she lived better, did work she loved, married a
wonderful man, and had a family. Nevertheless lack of
money felt like a constant issue. As her spiritual work
and practices deepened, as her relationship with God
expanded, she became gradually more grounded in a
deep sense of safety.

One day in a Yom Kippur guided meditation on forgive-
ness she received startling and extremely direct guidance: "You need to forgive yourself for worrying about
money . . . and from this moment on, you are to consider any anxiety in that area a sin." Carrie was taken aback
at the forcefulness of this instruction. But she could also
feel the truth of it. She understood that this word "sin"
was really just referring to a spiritual error. There were
subtle ways she was indulging old habits, specifically
negative thoughts and fears, that she had by now truly
outgrown. She came to understand that indulging in
these old ways was no longer a worthy use of her consciousness. Working with this guidance, she discovered
that there was a place on the left side inside her body
that actually closed down when she started running
through her old beliefs about there never being enough
and not getting what you need. Through this feeling
sense of what was happening with her consciousness,
she learned that when she shut down inside, it literally
closed down the flow of the universe to her. Which of
course would then confirm her negative beliefs that

there wasn't enough. As she worked with keeping herself open, more and more abundance flowed in—through work, inheritance, gifts, and many other unexpected ways and means. She reduced her working hours so that she could raise her children with spaciousness. In spite of the fact that her husband had a public service job with a minimal salary, they both had enough money. Her faith was truly justified and the old wounding she carried from her family was finally deeply healed. As the guidance indicated, all is well.

Questions for Meditation and Journal Work

1. Consider that your problems exist because you have somewhere violated Divine law. In that respect, could your problems be Divine gifts that clearly show you aspects of yourself that need to be transformed?

2. Sit for a moment and calmly consider your worries, conflicts, and problems. Consider that these worries, conflicts, and problems are important messages that are being constantly given to you. Consider that these messages are God's gifts pointing you in the direction of both fulfillment and abundance. Feel the ways you have been ignoring these messages. Feel the ways you have been trying to escape from the worries, conflicts, and problems. Can you feel your resistance to looking into the true meaning of these same worries, conflicts, and problems?

3. Are you willing to consider the possibility that disadvantageous or unpleasant events and circumstances need not interfere with your happiness? Are you open to viewing them as stepping stones that bring you that much closer to freedom and enlightenment?

4. Do you know the excruciating pain of not knowing why a painful event or situation exists in your life? Can you feel the pain associated with a life without meaning? When it comes to your own life, are you ready to start correlating cause and effect?

5. Consider that all suffering comes from your own negativity and destructiveness. See how you deny, evade, and repress this part of yourself. Can you see how unawareness of this same negativity and destructiveness prevents you from being aware of the ways it manifests in your life?

Opening to the Benign Nature of Life

"The grace of God is [everywhere]. It exists at all time, penetrating all that is. It exists in the very nature of ultimate reality, which is thoroughly benign. Grace means that all must work out for the best, no matter how evil, how painful, how tragic it may appear at the moment. In the end, when these negative experiences are fully assimilated and lived through by man, he comes full circle to the light of life, truth, joy, peace, pleasure supreme, eternal life, and well-being in all respects. This must always be the ultimate reality and therein lies grace. So, truly, you cannot help but live in the grace of God. The very air you breathe is permeated with it. Every substance of life, on all levels—from the finest vibrations and radiations to the crudest matter—is permeated with it. . . . You live and move your being in a universe that consists of such tenderness, such love, such personal care of the living God, and of the eternal presence in all that is, that it simply defies description. You are surrounded by a universe in which there is simply nothing ever to fear—no matter what momentary appearance may be!"

(Pathwork Guide Lecture 250)

Affirmation

My experience of the state of grace, my faith in the life process, is covered over by distorted interpretations, limited views, faulty outlooks, and personal blocks. I use every disharmony to help me release this state of grace, this faith in life, that is already inside me.

Ellen's Story

Ellen moved into a residential spiritual center in 1997 for what she thought would be one year of training in a foreign country. After she became a member of the community, she knew she had found her spiritual home. Her work assignment suited her, and people said that it was right that she was there. She loved the caring she could give to and receive from others. In 1998 her passport visa was about to expire, and this meant that she would have to leave the country where the center was located. In an effort to stay in the country, she filed an application with the government to be naturalized as a permanent resident. Because the number of people wishing to be naturalized far exceeded the quota, the odds were not in her favor when it came to remaining a resident at the center. She was soon thereafter delighted when her application was approved. Three months later she experienced the most traumatic month of her life. Her daughter, her only child, committed suicide. How she felt when she got the news is hard to describe, but at that time she could hardly breathe at all. To this day she still can't find the words to express the depth of her despair about the suicide, nor can she find the words to express her gratitude for the way people at the center supported her. All the spiritual teachings of this center seemed to have been demonstrated at this very painful time. The day she got notice of the suicide, the community collectively prayed for her, and her spiritual teacher stayed with her the entire day so that she could process her feelings and would not go into shock. Other people arranged Ellen's trip back to her country of origin so that she could attend the funeral. That evening, many members of the community gathered with her in the sanctuary building to comfort her and also to celebrate her daughter's life. Without all the unconditional support and love from other members of the community, she would be a different person today. It was as though God said: "Since she has agreed to go through this tremendous task, let's put her in the best possible spot for her healing." After she returned from her native country and from her daughter's funeral, she was dismayed to learn that the center was to soon be closed. Although she later lost the center and the community she loved so much, she appreciated how they both had been there for her when she most needed them.

Questions for Meditation and Journal Work

1. Are you open to the possibility that God's grace simply exists, that you do not have to do something to be worthy to receive it? If you don't believe this, do you see how this might interfere with your experience of grace? Do you have other beliefs or attitudes that might prevent you from experiencing the ever-present state of God's grace?

2. Consider that you now have both grace and faith inside yourself. Consider that your personal spiritual path involves releasing these states of consciousness so that you experience them on a regular and recurring basis. How would your life look if you didn't need to wait for grace and faith to be provided from the outside?

3. The bringing of light to situations of confusion and darkness involves grace. Consider that you spread grace when you become a messenger of light, truth, and love. What in your life would change if you acted as though you intentionally spread grace to other people?

4. Is it possible that your task is to surge into the world of matter, filling this world with Divine consciousness? Could it be that, as a part of this process, you have temporarily lost connection with both God and the state defined in the quote at the beginning of this chapter?

5. Consider that God, among other things, is truth. Consider that when you surrender to the truth, you are also surrendering to God. How might your insistence on having things your own way (that is, consistent with your self-will) interfere with your experience of God's will? Could your difficulty opening to God's will interfere with your openness to the already-existing grace of life?

*D*ay 21

Understanding Life's Feedback

"When you are unhappy, fearful, discouraged, in darkness, know at least that you are not in truth. This will make a lot of difference. Know that your blocks, your faulty vision, have separated you from the grace of God in which you swim, even now, although you do not know it."

(Pathwork Guide Lecture 250)

Affirmation

I commit to examining everything inside me, even those areas where I am most resistant, even those areas where I am afraid to look. I request Divine assistance in this process so that I can change, so that I can come into alignment with the truth.

Bernice's Story

As a small child, Bernice had an imaginary friend who she played with under a living room chair. She would lovingly talk to her friend and act as though her friend really did exist. This behavior scared Bernice's mother, because there had been some insanity in the family. When Bernice was about five years of age, her mother told her she had to stop having conversations with her friend, told her that she had to grow up and live in the world of reality. Although Bernice felt as though her friend was as real as anything else, she sadly agreed to follow her mother's instructions, in part out of her desire to protect her mother. When Bernice was 26, a friend told her she was a channel, a medium, and that she had a gift that could be used to help other people. When she heard these words, she felt comforted; she knew that this special gift was to be used, not to be ignored. From that point forward she opened up to her own spiritual existence by avidly pursuing meditation, prayer, crystals, and many other ways to connect with the unseen world. Soon thereafter she surrendered to who she was, and openly and publicly acknowledged that she had a talent for communicating with the spirit world. Again and again it seemed as though Bernice had spirit guides metaphorically tapping her on the shoulder, as if to say that they had information for her to pass along to other people. The joy this brought to her was immeasurable. These days Bernice is a professional guided intuitive counselor. This new avocation has brought her abundance and pleasure, and has allowed her to relax into who she really is. Her new role allows her to help people see where they are in their own healing journeys, as well as how to interpret prior experiences in light of the spiritual lessons that need to be learned. This feels consistent with God's will, instead of her own self-will, which was previously concerned with living up to the expectations of others. These days Bernice acknowledges that the imaginary friend was really a manifestation of her channel, and she no longer feels as though she must live by other people's standards.

Questions for Meditation and Journal Work

1. Are you denying some part of who you really are because you think it may be evil, sinful, or otherwise undesirable? Are you open to the possibility that this too may be a Divine manifestation, but that it has been distorted by wrong concepts and/or wrong perception?

2. Consider that whenever there is a misconception or an error, an out-of-balance situation is created. How might the out-of-balance aspects of your life be an indication of misconceptions or errors?

3. Consider that a lack of peace in your life is an indication that you have withheld a part of your soul from God and that you want to bargain with God. What part in you thinks you know better than God, thinks that in some way it would be a disadvantage to give yourself entirely to God?

4. Are you willing to entertain the possibility that there is a distinct difference between the laws of men and the laws of God? If so, assuming that the laws of God lead to constructive, loving, and joyous experience, how might you be violating the laws of God?

5. Think back over the last day, and in your mind's eye, re-create those few situations that were troublesome to you. How might your trouble with those situations be an indication that you are violating the truth, or perhaps living in a manner inconsistent with Divine law?

Feeling All Your Feelings

"The fulfillment which the universe has in store for you is not separate and far away from you, my friends. It is not in the distant future, not in a state beyond your physical life, not in attaining something through arduous means. It lies solely in the acknowledgement of what you really feel and think at this moment. It is this great simplicity that seems so hard to comprehend. You go through such pathetically unnecessary struggle in order to turn in the wrong direction, hoping against hope to find salvation without meeting yourself in the now." (Pathwork Guide Lecture 133)

Affirmation

As a human being, I acknowledge those parts of me that are fallible, irrational, needy, weak, vulnerable, wrong, and unhappy. In the space of acceptance that this creates, I allow myself to feel all my feelings and think all my thoughts.

Janette's Story

For six years, Janette has been dedicated to a rigorous path to illuminate her feelings, the truth of her situation, and the ways that she could grow spiritually. This work included private sessions with a spiritual teacher, meditation, prayer, yoga, and various courses on developing herself. This work has been the source of many revelations for her. For example, she examined the fact that, in all of her relationships with men, she was always the one to leave first. She saw that, by leaving first, she was protecting herself from being rejected. She was also surprised to see how she had consistently chosen to be with men who were cold and undemonstrative. She now appreciates how her choices in men were a re-creation of her childhood, which was emotionally barren. With all her ideas about relationship in upheaval, combined with the openness to truly see what she had been doing, she prayed for a new partner who was emotionally mature and communicative. Soon after she had enrolled in a new educational course on relationships, she got a call from Mark, a man she had met one week before. This was the man she had been waiting for. Over the following year, Janette and Mark have supported each other at a very deep spiritual and emotional level. They have been able to express things they had never before expressed, and also hear things the other said—things they had never before heard. They have released each other from unreasonable demands based on the past and have come to appreciate each other in much more truthful and grounded ways. For example, they now appreciate how they had repressed certain parts of themselves, exaggerated other parts of themselves, and failed to reveal still other parts of themselves. They are feeling more grounded now that they have gone through much of their childhood pain, and in the process, they have discovered some additional misconceptions about intimate relationship. They have both found their right to have their needs met, as well as the fact that they are lovable just as they are now. Janette and Mark have made a lifelong commitment to be together with love, growth, pleasure, and mutual support. A few months from now they will be married. With an expansive and radiant smile, Janette says that she is just starting to manifest the ways in which their lives are going to be a success.

Questions for Meditation and Journal Work

1. Consider that feeling your real pain is the gateway to pleasure and fulfillment. In meditation, say to yourself: "I would like to know, experience, and feel what I really feel." Notice if you attempt to talk yourself out of a feeling because you suspect irrationality. Notice whether you are talking yourself into building a case. Both of these are indications of an overly active mind.

2. Consider that the fear of feeling what is inside of you is the sole source of all destructiveness. The fear of experiencing your feelings causes you to be cruel and greedy, arrogant and isolated, selfish and life denying. With the Pathwork process introduced by this book, you convert constructive energy into destructive energy. Turning this around, you can convert destructive energy into constructive energy by feeling your real feelings. What implications might this have for you?

3. Consider how you avoid going into the truth of who you are, your feelings, and your thoughts. Do you, for example, adopt rules, theories, teachings, and other externally provided knowledge as a way to avoid going deeper into yourself? What else might you be doing to avoid going deeper with yourself?

4. Can you remember a time when, after significant withholding, you finally told the truth about what you felt or thought? Can you remember what a relief it was to be in truth?

5. Every child feels like he or she was not sufficiently loved. As a result, unless these feelings have deeply examined, deeply felt, and thereby come to terms with,

every adult still has feelings of hurt and pain left over from childhood. Consider that there is still part of you that is seeking to re-create similar circumstances so that you can now experience what you lacked as a child. How could the unconscious part of you that wants to re-create similar circumstances be interfering with the conscious part of you that seeks something quite different?

*D*ay 23

Believing in Your Own Potentials

"Your own potentials to experience beauty, joy, pleasure, love, wisdom, and creative expression, my dearest friends, are indeed infinite. . . . How deeply do you know that this is a reality? How deeply do you believe in your innermost potential to be self-creating, to be in bliss, to live the infinite life? How much do you believe in your resources to solve all your problems? How much do you trust in the possibilities that are not yet manifest? How much do you believe it is real that new vistas of yourself can be discovered? How much do you truly believe that you can unfold qualities of peace, coupled with excitement, of serenity coupled with adventure, through which life becomes a string of beauty even though initial difficulties are still to be overcome? How much do you really believe in all this, my friends?"

(Pathwork Guide Lecture 183)

Affirmation

> *I can withstand the disappointment and upset associated with my current situation. There are many possible alternative situations that I have the power to manifest, and the current situation need not be carried forward into the future.*

Werner and Sherry's Story

In 1989, while visiting friends in California, Werner and Sherry decided to follow a 15-year longing to move from Michigan to California. In 1990, as their youngest child graduated from high school and headed for college, they bought a home in California and put their Michigan home on the market. Werner and Sherry were convinced they needed this change, even though it meant they both would give up well-established psychotherapy practices in metropolitan Detroit. Five days later, Iraq invaded Kuwait. This was unsettling, but in planning the move to San Diego, Sherry expected to take a job offered to her as director of an after-school arts program for children. Similarly, Werner planned to do management consulting based on his years of experience in business and psychology. After arriving in San Diego six months later, Werner discovered that there was no consulting work to be found, because the entire region was suffering from a major cutback in government defense contractor spending coupled with an economic slowdown. Sherry found her job was not what had been promised, and she decided to leave it. The United States was preparing for the Gulf War, and the Michigan real estate market was at a virtual standstill. They had two mortgages, two children to support in expensive private colleges, and no jobs. Despite their faith, they were afraid. Many things had happened to facilitate their move to California. They trusted that this move was right, but they could see their savings flowing away. Originally, they had planned to be part-time spiritual counselors when they were not doing their regular jobs. Ultimately, they wanted to establish a regional spiritual center in California. Prospects for any type of work were bleak, and their financial resources would, at this rate, soon be exhausted. What could they do? After deeply meditating and praying to know God's will, they let go in trust, deciding to give all their time and energy to starting the new spiritual center. Within days, an environmentalist from Alaska called to say he wanted to do an 11-day spiritual intensive with them, and then other people asked them to lead ongoing workshops in both Los Angeles and San Francisco. Werner and Sherry lived on an austerity budget for a while, but they felt very alive and supported in many ways. Their fears diminished as they followed their calling, and they trusted that their finances would somehow work out. In their second year in California, doing only spiritual work, their income was greater than it had ever been in Michigan.

Questions for Meditation and Journal Work

1. Do you resist opening to the possibility that your potentials are infinite, that your capacity to create the life you want grows as you do your own spiritual work?

2. Do you believe that some good fortune you experienced in the past was a fluke, a random act of forces outside yourself? Or do you see it as a reflection of your ability to create?

3. Consider that, to the degree that you live up to your potential, to that same degree will your life be a dynamic, full, and pleasurable experience. At this point in time, in what way are you not yet living up to your potential?

4. If you keep some part of yourself in an untruthful state, you do not enter into a state where you are wholeheartedly committed to aligning with your God-consciousness. If you are not willing to give over to your God-consciousness, then you cannot experience your God-given power to create the life you want. What might be the untruthful state you don't yet want to let go of?

5. Consider that the ability to create everything you need and want is already within you, that you are already perfectly prepared to create the life you desire. Consider that you have temporarily moved away from that state, and that your spiritual task is to once again rediscover who you really are. How does this make you feel?

Transforming Duality into Unity

"In a deeper sense, there are no contradictions at all. It is utterly possible to rejoice in worldly fulfillments as expressions of inner states, while no longer straining toward one state and away from another. This attitude can exist only when you deeply know that ultimately there is the reality of God, there is life eternal and there is fulfillment and well-being in every possible way. Because you have attained a state without straining, you glimpse and finally experience this outer reality. It is equally true to state that you can relinquish the straining because you glimpse this state. It must be approached from both ends." (Pathwork Guide Lecture 253)

Affirmation

Through my commitment to utterly know and grow toward God, I am increasingly experiencing the happiness that is mine for the asking. I no longer need to struggle between one form of fulfillment and another.

Diana's Story

Diana learned a strong work ethic and the importance of caring for other people from her father. Her father was generous and caring with his employees, and they loved him for it. As an adult, Diana spent 19 years working for a school district, going from classroom teacher to special educator to the director of special education programs. After that, she ran a summer camp for girls, and later a yoga studio. Although these jobs didn't pay a great deal, she has always felt comfortable with money and has always believed that the universe will continue to support her. She never felt she had to worry about money. With this attitude, she has been considerate and loving with her employees, and that has helped to make her jobs a pleasure. Although Diana lives in a relatively poor community, where many people have significant fears about money, she has been forthcoming in her giving. As a result, she has repeatedly observed how she has gotten back more than she contributed. For example, with the summer camp, she needed to invest a lot of her own money. But the camp continued to provide a nurturing place for young women to realize their potential, so it grew and eventually became self-sustaining. Although she sold the camp for a loss, all the money she invested in the camp and then some came back to her when she sold a house that she owned. Separately, this same attitude of abundance and unification was evident while she was the summer camp director. In that capacity, it occurred to her that she needed an assistant. The assistant needed to have an unusual combination of talents and skills. Specifically, the assistant needed to know a lot about both horses and bookkeeping, be great with kids, and be a good manager. Without much advertising or effort, she let it be known among her friends that she was looking for an assistant. Soon thereafter, a woman with all the necessary qualifications contacted Diana. Diana already knew and respected this woman from prior business dealings, and the woman was very interested in the position. This woman was so perfect for the job that when Diana sold the camp, some 12 years ago, the assistant continued to work for the camp, and continues to work there to this day.

Questions for Meditation and Journal Work

1. Consider that only a very healthy, integrated, harmonious, and happy person can really love, help, and give to others. In the interests of being of greater service to both others and God, are you willing to improve your own life?

2. Have you cut yourself off, outwardly or inwardly, from other people? If so, are you ready to give up the separating attitude that isolates you? Are you ready to give to, and be given to, by other people?

3. Does your ambition cause you to become ruthless with other people? In other words, does the manifestation of your desire come at the expense of other people? If so, can you see how the manifestation of your desire can only rob you of inner peace?

4. It is not selfish to pray for the insight, strength, and ability to remove the obstacles you have placed between yourself and happiness. It is not selfish to work on yourself so that you more clearly see your errors and ignorance. It is not selfish to feel your true feelings and to use these feelings as spiritual stepping stones to the realization of your own happiness. How do you feel about these assertions?

5. Is there a part of you that believes you are either rich or poor? Consider that this perspective is nothing more than a comparison that is concerned with appearance values. Consider adopting a more unified approach, where everything in your life is moving you toward a more abundant, happy, and enlightened state.

Feeling Your Gratitude

"Compassion and love, gratitude for the beauty of creation, appreciation of and joy about it must also create a deep pain when something is destroyed, a pain that needs to be suffered. This pain is ever so different from the neurotic pain, the pain by association, the pain of masochistic self-punishment that identifies with what appears to be a victim. This living, loving, healthy pain is also the threshold to joy and ecstasy. . . . As long as this pain is denied, the price becomes much higher, for such pain must turn against whoever has inflicted it, or against whoever colludes with those who inflict the pain by passively standing by. Many self-defeating patterns are connected with pain you have unwittingly inflicted because you have not let yourself know and feel them."   (Pathwork Guide Lecture 252)

Affirmation

I open all of my channels of feeling and sensing, and, as a result, I experience my fulfillment, awe, wonder, and gratitude.

Amy's Story

Amy was absolutely terrified of the pain and difficulty associated with change, and as a result, she had stayed in the same job as a management recruiter for many years, even though she hated it. For the last four years, Amy had been studying part-time to be a hands-on healer. She didn't have much money and she wondered how she was going to support herself when and if she were to build an independent practice as a healer. This fear didn't deter her from completing the training, because she felt called to work as a healer. The time for her graduation from the healing school came to pass, and she went away to a distant city for the ceremony. When she returned to her home, she was surprised to learn that she had been laid off from her management recruiter job with a significant severance package. If she had done what she thought she would have to do, which was to just quit this job, there would have been no severance package and no unemployment insurance. Now she got to enjoy both of these streams of income while she built her new healing practice. The timing was perfect, and to her it felt as it was more than just a coincidence. Amy doubts she would ever have gone into business for herself if the layoff hadn't taken place. This incident has caused her to reexamine the way she looks at change. She is now considering that change might be both natural and safe. The incident has also prompted her to think again about her relationship to the healthy pain that goes along with the destruction of obsolete ways of thinking and looking at life. She wonders whether she had been too afraid of this pain that accompanies the changes we really want to make in our lives. While she still worries about money as she gets her new healing practice off the ground, she has a lot of gratitude for the synchronicity of her current situation.

Questions for Meditation and Journal Work

1. Do you feel that if you receive something from other people you will be unduly obligated to them? Does an attitude like this prevent you from being open to receiving? If you harbor such a misconception, ask yourself why you believe this, why you cannot simply feel your gratitude?

2. Can you remember an event in your past for which you had immense gratitude? Can you remember how you approached that situation? Could this same successful approach be used to manifest the abundance you seek?

3. Consider the possibility that every person is a Divine manifestation. Consider that we all have forgotten or turned away from this fact in one way or another. If we are all Divine manifestations, each showing up in our own way, then nobody is inferior and nobody is superior. Can you feel this as a possibility? Can you feel your gratitude for the beauty and wonder that other people truly are?

4. Do you feel guilty when you enjoy life, when you are grateful for the good things in your life? If so, investigate why you feel this guilt. Consider that when you are really honest with yourself, when you are feeling your true feelings, and when you are taking self-responsibility, then the enjoyment of these positive things is healthy and positive (then there is no need for the guilt).

5. Have you come to the point in your life where you would like to give something back to God out of your gratitude? While this giving may at first seem like a hardship and a sacrifice, can you consider that it will become the greatest joy imaginable?

Day 26

Releasing Victimization and Hopelessness

"When you feel unhappy or hopeless, question yourself: "Do I not have another way to react to this situation that seems to befall me out of nowhere and to which I choose to react negatively, destructively, making myself hopeless, complaining and feeling angry about it?" This choice is yours. Your anger and complaints against the world are wasted, for all that energy could do so much to build new life for you if it were used properly. You cannot change others, but you can certainly change your own attitudes and your thinking. Then life offers its limitless possibilities to you."

(Pathwork Guide Lecture 174)

Affirmation

I choose to let go of victimization and hopelessness, adopting instead the way to a new life through self-responsibility and constructive change.

Mark's Story

Mark was a bitter recovering alcoholic who had recently gone through a divorce from his wife of 20 years. He hoped that stopping his drinking would allow him to deal with his feelings about the divorce. It didn't turn out that way. For three months he stayed alone in what seemed, now that his wife was gone, like a cavernous big house way out in the country. Because he was retired, he had plenty of time to wallow in his anger, his resentments, his self-pity, and his sense of hopelessness about life. He prayed to be able to deal with his feelings, but he had no idea of how he was going to be able to do it. Since he lived on a meager pension, he had no extra money for a therapist or self-help courses. Mark seemed peculiarly trapped in a downward spiral. His continued prayers opened him to the possibility that things could change for the better, and he had the urge to go to a square dance, even though he wasn't in the best physical shape. At the dance he met a red-haired woman who was particularly interesting. The way she acted was different—she was happy and free. Mark asked her how she got to be that way, and she eagerly told him about a spiritual path based on self-responsibility, telling the truth, and living in the moment. After the dance she sent him some written material about this spiritual path, and he was quite moved when he read it. But because he had such a limited income, he couldn't attend any of the courses or events offered by the organization following this spiritual path. He continued his prayers for assistance in working through his feelings about the divorce and was pleasantly surprised a few days later when his ex-employer called him and offered him a part-time consulting job. This option had never occurred to him, because he had thought he was too old to get a job, that nobody would hire him. With the extra money this job provided, he went on to take several courses with the organization, to heal his feelings about his divorce, and to appreciate an intimate connection with many others who pursued the same spiritual path.

Questions for Meditation and Journal Work

1. Do you feel hopeless about having a meaningful and rewarding life because, deep down inside, you do not feel deserving? And if you don't feel deserving, is it because you don't like certain traits you have? If you think you are these undesirable traits, you will certainly despair; but if you think you have come to this earth to heal these same traits, then hope is truly justified.

2. Your feelings of being injured by life circumstances can appear to be quite real. Are you willing to probe more deeply, to perhaps discover that they are in fact not real at all? Are you willing to consider the possibility that these feelings are a cultivated habit, and that they can be changed?

3. Are you wrapped up in a repeating cycle of resentment, accusation, blame, and self-justifying victim consciousness? Are you denying the role you have in the creation of your life circumstances?

4. Are you willing to honestly face yourself as you are right now? Can you muster the courage and humility to confront the poverty consciousness you have created in certain areas of your life? By clearly seeing this creation of yours, by feeling the pain of it, you will tunnel through to a new point where you can sense the ultimate benign nature of life, a place where life wants to give you exactly what you need.

5. Consider that life is inherently characterized by movement and change. Have you instead assumed that life is fixed, that things will always be the way they are now? If you have an assumption about the fixedness of life,

about how things will continue to be the way they are now, how does this limit your perspective about what could come next?

Taking Personal Responsibility

"You are never, never dependent on another person, even if
it seems that way. That is the illusion of the world of manifestation. The teachings of the Path I show you must prove
to you forever more that it is you yourself who inflict difficulties, conflicts, and hurts on yourself, no matter how
much the other person may be at fault. If you are free of
images, illusions, wrong conclusions, and wrong concepts,
the wrong deeds of others can never affect you."

(Pathwork Guide Lecture 52)

Affirmation

*I open to the possibility that I am ultimately
responsible for my experience of life, and that,
with this attitude, there is no need for
self-pity, resignation, passive endurance, or
resentments against life.*

Paul's Story

Paul grew up with a narcissistic, bipolar, and occasionally violent father. His father could fly into a rage at the
slightest provocation, and often for no apparent reason.
As a way to protect himself, Paul would try to stay out of
the limelight, would try to be as quiet and unobtrusive as
possible. Although his father had died years ago, as an
adult in his 40s, Paul was still isolated and socially with-
drawn. Although he intellectually knew it was not true,
emotionally he felt like his father was lurking in the next

room. He worried that the people around him would act like his father, would all of a sudden flip out and get violent, even if he had known these same people for years. The trauma of his childhood haunted him, and he continued to get exceedingly uncomfortable whenever somebody would get angry and yell. In an effort to get to a place where he could trust life, Paul embarked on an extensive program of self-discovery and self-improvement. Through this work he was dismayed to see how he was empowering the memory of his father, how he was letting his father's image rule his life. He additionally saw how his fear of unpredictable violence was distancing him from people, causing him to feel genuinely comfortable only when he was alone. Paul asked his spiritual community for assistance with this deep-seated fear, and in the process revealed his distrust to every person present at a large event. He did this out of his commitment to transform himself, even though it felt embarrassing and juvenile for him to have this problem. The community prayed for his healing, and that very instant he felt an electrifying surge of energy move through him. In the weeks that followed he was surprised to notice that he was enjoying the presence of other people, that he was feeling a loving connection with other people, and that he was considerably less afraid of sudden violence. As he gradually became more trusting of life and other people, he opened his heart and established more intimate relationships. Perhaps the greatest example of this is his relationship with a new girlfriend, which has been characterized by many experiences of love and bliss instead of his previously encountered experiences of fear and distrust. He now revels in the pleasure of deeply connecting with other people and can't imagine going back to the isolated and lonely life he used to lead.

Questions for Meditation and Journal Work

1. If you are profoundly affected by other people's negativity, explore why you are so vulnerable. Are you on some level denying self-responsibility and insisting on blaming others for your misery?

2. Remember how you responded to a recent negative event. Become aware of how you hardened yourself, how you numbed yourself, how you emotionally contracted in response to this event. Then accept that you do this. Now, can you envision another way to respond where you are open and receptive, where you can deal with both the negative event and the negative feelings that accompany it?

3. Humans try to avoid painful experiences, and in the process they often make themselves more prone to such experiences. Are you willing to adopt a more accepting attitude, where you are able to endure a little pain? Are you able to take this to the next level, where you not only can endure some pain, but where you also can start to investigate how you may have caused the pain?

4. Consider that there is no power outside of yourself that determines the extent of your fulfillment or the extent of your pain. When it comes to the unpleasant aspects of your life, can you open to the possibility that you are not being punished by God, but that you are instead unwittingly violating some spiritual laws?

5. Consider that your guilt about your destructive self is more damaging than this same destructive self that you so despise. Do you use this guilt as an excuse not to get conscious about this part of yourself? Do you use this guilt as a way to avoid taking self-responsibility?

Dropping Blame

"Anyone who is on a path such as this and who makes a total commitment to truth, to self-facing, to self-purification, to giving up all defenses and all subterfuges in order to face that which seems most difficult and momentarily painful; anyone who chooses to forego the temptation to concentrate on the real or apparent wrongs of others so as to avoid the self, and who is thus committed to his growth above and beyond all other considerations in his life, will and must make the connection that will then also bring all outer and inner fulfillment." (Pathwork Guide Lecture 216)

Affirmation

Whenever I am upset about the faults of another, there must be something in me that is not right. I ask for Divine assistance with my efforts to illuminate that grain of sand in me that causes disharmony, rather than focusing on the mountain of wrong in another.

Meridith's Story

Meridith was scheduled to teach a course in Charleston, but she mistakenly booked an airplane ticket to Charlotte. She was not paying attention to the details and had not examined her ticket until after her bag had been checked in at the airport ticket counter. It was almost time to get on the plane when it occurred to her that she had made this mistake. She rushed up to the airline's gate agent and tried to change her ticket. The agent informed her that this was not possible so close to departure time, but that he could remove her bag from the airplane. The agent also informed her that a "same day" ticket to Charleston would cost $1,000. She was angry and frustrated that the gate agent apparently could not hear that she desperately needed to be in Charleston at 4:00 p.m. that same day. She then appreciated how this problem reminded her of her birth—she felt like she couldn't get out of the airport, just like she couldn't get out of the birth canal. She felt as though there were no choices open to her and that she would die. At that point she began to breathe deeply and she heard the voice of love. The voice told her that everything would work out, and that she needed this incident for her healing. Meridith then appreciated how she was behaving in a habitual way, allowing herself to be the important child. Deciding to be an adult, she asked to see the gate agent's supervisor. When the supervisor arrived, she was surprised to see that his first name was Arcangel. She viewed his unusual name as another invitation to let go of the hand of fear, to know that God is always present when we are willing to be present in the moment. As she talked to the supervisor, she felt her anxiety disappear, and she once again inhabited her body. She explained that she had confused Charleston with Charlotte, that it was her own fault, not her travel agent's fault, and not the airline's fault. Arcangel arranged for Meridith to fly to Charleston through several other airports for an additional fare of only $81 round trip. The total travel time was 11 hours rather than what should have been 4 hours. The extra time she spent at airports was a meditation and a wonderful teaching about letting go and allowing God to do his work. Since this incident, she has noticed that her teaching is more relaxed and she definitely pays more attention to details.

She now sees the incident as an opportunity to take responsibility without defending or blaming.

Questions for Meditation and Journal Work

1. Even if you no longer overtly blame other people, and even if you no longer make sure you are cleared of all possible responsibility for negative situations, are you still blaming others deep inside yourself?

2. Consider that as long as you project your own darkness onto other people and situations, that you cannot appreciate and expand the God-consciousness within yourself. What does this bring up for you?

3. Can you see how your self-hate causes you to blame others? Can you feel how the more you blame others, the less of a grip you have on reality and truth? Can you feel how the more you lose a grip on reality and truth, the more you hate yourself?

4. If you blame others, and you acknowledge that part of you that wants to blame, can you also see a part in you that desires not to blame? When you are in touch with the latter part, can you sense the part of you that desires to clearly and truthfully see both the good and the bad—in both yourself and in others? Can you see how the truth never leads to blame?

5. Consider that by blaming others, you bring isolation, pain, and friction to your relationships. Consider that by taking self-responsibility, you create relationships characterized by joy, freedom, and productivity. What implications might this have for your life?

Using Positive Aggression

"Yet you also need to fight for those fulfillments by relinquishing your passivity, your irresponsibility in wanting an ideal authority to do it all for you. You need active, positive aggression to never allow the dark forces within you to conquer you, or make you believe that all is futile, or convince you to give in to their whisperings of hopelessness and false surrender. Here you must stand firm and realize the power embedded in your thought processes, in your inner will, in your ability to chose faith over fear, courage over cowardice. For what requires more courage than believing in God's truth and your power to live and demonstrate it?"   (Pathwork Guide Lecture 254)

Affirmation

I use my own positive aggression to move out, expand, improve, and create, just as I use this positive aggression to confront negativity, injustice, and abuse.

Nadine's Story

Nadine was born and raised in a Middle Eastern country. About 15 years ago, she moved to the United States to live with her American husband. After only seven years in the states, she separated from her husband with the intention to create a new life. This was a difficult undertaking, because English was not her native language, she had very little money, and she had joint custody of their five-year-old daughter. In the divorce, she gave up her rights to alimony and child support, because she understood that both she and her ex-husband would contribute to the support of their daughter with the best of intentions. From her parents Nadine had received some very traditional views about the roles of men and women. For example, her mother was always second in importance to her father and always depended on his authority. As a single parent, Nadine felt insecure, because she did not have a man to depend on. To make her situation more difficult, her ex-husband was intimidating and uncooperative whenever she saw him, and he was not paying his share of their daughter's support. In the years that followed, Nadine established a wonderful and intimate relationship with her daughter, and this helped give Nadine a sense of security as a good mother. At the same time, Nadine still felt as though her ex-husband was the "supreme authority" in all matters related to their daughter. Operating with this image, Nadine was afraid to confront her ex-husband about not contributing his fair share. She felt betrayed because he wasn't living up to his promise and helpless to change the situation. About six years ago, she discovered a powerful spiritual path that helped her connect to that part in her that was assertive and God connected. With the support of a good friend, a caring lover, and a spiritual teacher, she started exploring her fear of authority. Without this deep spiritual work, she would never have spoken up, taken her ex-husband to court, and eventually received a court order instructing him to pay more child support. Even though the additional amount was small, the process helped her come out of a victim mind-set and helped her confront her ex-husband's dominant and uncooperative behavior. Her personal transformation also shifted her relationship with her ex-husband so that he now treats her with greater respect.

Questions for Meditation and Journal Work

1. Consider that positive aggression involves an energetic, positive, and life-affirming movement that is grounded in the truth, in fairness, and in what is right for all concerned. In your fight for sought-after fulfillments, do you employ positive aggression?

2. Can you bring your positive aggression to bear on the evil (unevolved parts) within you? Can you assert the positive forces within and around you by exposing and confronting those parts of yourself that are negative and destructive?

3. In terms of your desired abundance, are you exposing and confronting the things that are unfair and/or abusive?

4. Is the decision to stand up and assert yourself versus giving in and following along made from a place of your conscious mind? Is it made from a place of deep inner knowing, a place where God speaks to you? Or is it made from some other place?

5. Do you have an image that says a good person is meek, passive, and unassertive? If so, how could this be holding you back from creating your sought-after fulfillments?

Finding Strength to Change Your Life

"And if you wish it, you will receive the necessary strength. No matter how busy you are in your life, you will have time, not only to fulfill your duties as you have done before, but infinitely better. And you will have time to enjoy life, but infinitely better too, when you lose the fear and insecurity that constantly lives in your soul and spoils everything for you so much, my dear ones. And do not think you will not have the strength to do the necessary work on this path; this strength will be given to you drop by drop for all your needs—spiritual and material—if you first make the decision for it and trust that God will give you what you need for it."

(Pathwork Guide Lecture 26)

Affirmation

The Divine source that created the universe is accessible deep within me. This forever-moving and forever-expanding source has the power to change anything. This source is available whenever I deliberately contact it.

Elaine's Story

Five years ago, Elaine, a sports medicine physical therapist, was recently divorced with three children to feed and $287 to her name. At that time, she had a vivid and compelling dream that she would one day have her own healing clinic. Soon thereafter, to avoid rush-hour traffic, she turned down a street she did not know and discovered a building with a sign out front that said "For Lease." The building looked exactly like the clinic in her dreams. On a lark Elaine called the rental agent, who encouraged her to fill out an application to lease the building even though she had virtually no money. She was leaving on vacation three days later. Provided the owners approved of her as a lessee, the rental agent said that Elaine would have to commit to the space, if she really wanted it, within that three-day period. To supplement her limited income, Elaine occasionally worked as an attendant at a bingo parlor, but she was not scheduled to work that evening. Later that afternoon, she received a call at home that the bingo parlor was shorthanded and they wanted her to work that evening. At the parlor Elaine was surprised when an acquaintance approached her and offered to loan her $10,000, no strings attached, so that she could take the lease. The woman who made the offer was not a friend, so Elaine didn't really believe that her offer was anything more than a gesture of goodwill. On the morning of the day when she was scheduled to leave on her vacation, Elaine called the rental agent and left a disappointed voice mail message saying that she could not take the lease. However, the rental agent had already left town on a business trip and did not get Elaine's message. That afternoon, Elaine was again surprised to get a call from the woman she had met at bingo, who indicated she had a check ready for Elaine to pick up. When she met with the woman, Elaine felt acknowledged and trusted, because the woman didn't want a promissory note or anything in writing, she didn't want interest, and she didn't want the note to be paid back at any particular time. Instead, the woman simply told Elaine that she should pay it back when she could. At that point, feeling elated, Elaine then called the owners of the building and arranged to lease it. Today she has a thriving clinic with five professionals and has long since paid back the $10,000. Elaine is convinced that some angels were looking after her and that she clearly received Divine support in the manifestation of her dream.

Questions for Meditation and Journal Work

1. Consider the possibility that all your needs will be met if you surrender completely to the will of God, if you are committed to your own life's purpose, and if you are determined to live in truth. Could your unwillingness to give in this manner be interfering with your ability to receive what you say you want?

2. Are your desired fulfillments a reflection of your ego's desire, or are they a reflection of God's will (your life purpose)? Consider that, as long as these desires are a reflection of your limited ego, then you will not be able to trust that life is benign and deeply supportive of your endeavors. Consider that, if your desires are a reflection of Divine will, then they will be truly connected not only with others but also with the universe, and then they will naturally be abundantly forthcoming.

3. Consider that a healthy acceptance of both truth and the nature of life will provide you with additional strength. Consider that God will provide what you need to fulfill your life's task. After a pause for reflection, can you see how you might be off course in the fulfillment of your life's task?

4. In your concern about getting your personal needs met, are you resisting your own soul's movement? Are

you resisting the movement of your inner being? If so, how is this nonmovement, this stagnation, this denial of your own personal process, preventing you from manifesting the life you want?

5. The child in all of us erroneously believes we can be happy only if our will is done. This causes us to have an underlying belief that we must always get what we want, or else we believe we can never get what we want. Either end of the spectrum is out of synch with reality. Reality involves getting some things we want and some things we don't. Can you see how you have been undermining your psychic strength with this illusion? Can you feel how you could have a deep inner peace, how you could enjoy new strength and confidence, if you were to embrace the reality of this world?

Understanding You Have Everything You Need

"What is the attitude you have toward the present difficulty? This is what counts. This is where you have a choice to assume a constructive or destructive attitude, a truthful or self-deceptive attitude. You have the power to find out what you really feel and why you feel it. You have the power to request guidance from the greatest wisdom conceivable, which is within yourself. You have the possibility to want to be on the constructive road that leads to creating and unfolding rather than giving up, as is done so often in a difficulty. You also have the power to let go of stubborn insistence and rigid upholding of unconscious attitudes whose nature is as yet unexplored. You have the power to overcome the temptation to indulge in resignation and self-pity. Therefore you have everything you need to assume the attitude to activate the greatest power in the universe. Each and every living instant—it doesn't matter whether it's beautiful or ugly, easy and lighthearted or difficult and heavy—contains the potential to be in bliss, provided you penetrate the Now to its deepest level. Each instant contains ultimate truth, if you want only to turn in the right direction." (Pathwork Guide Lecture 168)

Affirmation

I possess all the powers, faculties, and resources necessary to manifest what I truly need in life. It is only my misconceptions, my limited view, and fear of happiness that prevent me from seeing this truth.

David and Mary's Story

David and Mary had been living in a rent-controlled townhouse in one of the most desirable areas of a large city. After seven years, the landlord notified them that they were being evicted so that the landlord's son could live in the townhouse. David and Mary were shocked. The notice had come totally out "of the blue," especially because they had been model tenants. To them, it seemed so unfair. In their own words, they were "freaked-out" and consulted a lawyer to find out if there was some way to block the eviction. Abandoning a legal fight, they frantically started looking for another place to live. Over the years, they had occasionally discussed the possibility of moving, but had never felt ready. They didn't even know where in this same city they wanted to live or what their criteria for choosing a new place should be. While they had been in the townhouse, real estate prices had increased dramatically, but rent control laws had insulated them from this reality. While researching the real estate market, they were again shocked to find how much it would cost to rent another property comparable to the one in which they had been living. After much anguish, they decided they wanted something nice and that they were willing to pay a lot more than they had been paying for the townhouse. They were even willing to dip into retirement savings to pay rent for a short while, if that were necessary. After looking around for a few days, they were thrilled to find a single-family residence for rent. The place felt comfortable, so they moved in. After a few months at the new location, they were amazed at how much they loved the new area. While the house is smaller than their old townhouse, it is very close to a state park, it has clean air, the street is very quiet, and the neighborhood is safe.

David and Mary now feel the proximity to the moun-
tains, and they enjoy looking at the deer that occasionally wander into their backyard. Their business has recently picked up, so they haven't had to use any of their
retirement savings. While the transition was harsh and
abrupt, the universe was showing them that they
were ready for a change. They came to appreciate that
getting evicted turned out to be a blessing in disguise,
because they are so much happier in their new house
and location.

Questions for Meditation and Journal Work

1. As an adult, what are your real needs? Do these
include self-expression, personal growth, spiritual development, and reaching for one's potential? Do these
include love, pleasure, fulfillment, good relationships,
and making a meaningful contribution to life?

2. Do you have childhood real needs that were not
adequately fulfilled, needs that you nonetheless are
still holding onto? Do these include being taken care
of, needing to receive care, needing attention, and
being seen in your own uniqueness?

3. If your "needs" are presently unfulfilled the way you
want them to be, is the pain about this situation more
than just pain about the present? Is it also pain from the
past, pain from those times in your childhood
when you were frustrated by your parents or caretak-
ers? As you separate the present needs of your adult
from the past needs of your child, you will be increasingly able to bear the temporary frustration that must be
borne on the way to fulfillment.

4. How have your expectations about the future been limited by your past or present experience? Can you rigorously, actively, and dynamically create a vision of a future that goes beyond these limitations? What would it be like to inhabit such a future?

5. Do you want bliss because you fear pain? Do you want eternal life because you fear death? Do you want happiness because you fear unhappiness? If you answered "yes" to any of these questions, consider that your fear may block the attainment of what you desire. Consider that you may need to deeply feel your fear, and perhaps experience it as well, in order to realize that it is not nearly as bad as you imagined.

Discovering the Pathwork Community

The Pathwork material emphasizes that "no one is capable of doing this work alone."[1] Many of us refuse to see certain aspects of ourselves, but these aspects are readily observable by others. Certain things never occurred to us because we have misconceptions and erroneous images about life, but these same things can be readily identified by another person. If you are genuinely committed to doing the deep psychological and spiritual work necessary to transform yourself, to turn your life around, and to come closer to God, then you will be guided to one or more people who can help you.

One of the fastest ways to find people who are similarly committed to their own spiritual development, who can help you with your own spiritual path, is to attend a Pathwork course or event. These courses and events include lecture study classes, emotional process groups, weekend seminars, and year-long training programs. These courses and events are offered in a variety of countries throughout the world—you can get a sense for the current offerings and the worldwide Pathwork community by consulting the Pathwork Web site (www.pathwork.org).

Although most people are initially attracted to the Pathwork because the material deeply and profoundly speaks to their current condition and because the Pathwork holds the possibility of turning their life

---

[1] Pathwork Guide Lecture 40

around, once they become involved with the Pathwork, they become quite attached to the community. In this community, there is an aliveness, a vitality, and a dynamism that cannot be found elsewhere. This is readily observable in a lunchroom of Pathworkers—the room is loud and boisterous as many people joyfully and excitedly engage in deeply meaningful conversation.

Being with other people who are also committed to their own spiritual growth is a profound experience that defies words. When we support other people, we are in turn richly giving to ourselves. The Guide spoke to this experience:[2] "Your happiness will be given to you so that you can pass it on. Then you will indeed become a link in the chain, which is the sole requisite to keep the stream of happiness alive and flowing. In this way it will never dry out. Whatever the person who serves as such a link gives out will be reciprocated a hundredfold."

Dr. John Pierrakos, husband to Eva Pierrakos, said:[3] "I feel that everything is possible if I stay on my path. I also feel that all of us can perform miracles by being together and working together in truth, by giving to others what has been given to us." This is the great potential contribution of Pathwork community—to live authentically, to drop our masks, to love each other, and to open to the grace and beauty of life.

[2] Pathwork Guide Lecture 5
[3] Additional Material 13

Researching Specific Lecture References

A parenthetical abbreviation can be found at the end of each of the quotes found in this book. For example, the notation "(Pathwork Guide Lecture 236)" occurs on Day 16. This means that the quote can be found in Pathwork Guide Lecture number 236.

If one or more of the quotes in this book speaks to you, you are urged to read the entire lecture. Each of the lectures is approximately 10 pages long, often with a few additional pages of questions and answers. The lectures provide much more context and detail about the topics addressed in this book. The lectures additionally contain both encouragement and exceptional clarity about the psychological and spiritual issues we all face in everyday life.

Each of the lectures can be downloaded via the Internet. They are all Adobe Acrobat files that can be read on any type of computer (you may need to download a free copy of the Adobe Acrobat Reader program). The Pathwork community hopes that the easy access to these lectures will help people in all walks of life to benefit from these important teachings.

To download the lectures, go to www.pathwork.org. This site will provide you with more information about Pathwork workshops, the Pathwork community, and the Pathwork transformational process. Follow the prompts directing you to the Pathwork lectures. After several different screens, you will be presented with an index of the lectures. The lectures can then be downloaded directly from this screen.

Those wishing to do extensive study with the Pathwork lectures will probably want to buy the CD-ROM, which contains all of the lectures. The CD-ROM can be obtained from www.pathwork.org or by writing to Pathwork Press, PO Box 6010, Charlottesville, VA 22906 USA. For readers in the United States and Canada, Pathwork Press can be telephoned at 1-800-PATHWORK. One of the great benefits of having the CD-ROM is the ability to do a key word search across all of the lectures. For example, if you're dealing with the pain of a divorce, you could search for all references to the word "divorce." The CD-ROM also contains a rich text format (RTF) version of the Pathwork lectures, and this file format allows you to cut and paste specific quotes into other documents (please note the copyright notice appearing at the end of each lecture).

Yet another option for researching the lectures involves buying Pathwork books. These books condense and interpret material from the lectures. These books can also be purchased online at www.pathwork.org, from most booksellers, and from various Pathwork centers around the world. (A list of these regional centers can be found on this same web page.)

Meditation for Three Voices

You may be at a point in your life where you feel deeply conflicted, confused, and unable to move ahead productively. It is at these times that one specific type of meditation, called the meditation for three voices, can be a powerful technique to break through to a new level of understanding. This deeper understanding can, in turn, help define the course of action you should take. This chapter outlines the steps in this powerful meditation. Readers looking for more information about the technique are referred to the Pathwork lecture entitled The Process Of Meditation.[1]

There are three different levels of personality that all people have. The first is called the conscious ego. This level directs your daily activities. It is this level that includes your conscious knowing and willing. The second is the unconscious egotistical child, or your lower self. This level includes those parts of you that are still ignorant and destructive. It is this level that has claims to omnipotence. It is this level that insists on having its way, exactly the way it wants it, right now. The third is the higher self, or the universal self, that part of you that is connected with God. It is this level at which you can find your superior wisdom, your power, and your love, as well as your comprehensive understanding of your life on earth.

In this meditation, the ego activates both the lower self and the higher self. A constant interaction between these three levels is mediated by the ego, which acts as an impartial traffic cop. In this capacity, the ego

---

[1] Pathwork Guide Lecture 182—see chapter titled "Researching Specific Lecture References" for details.

needs to allow the lower self to reveal itself, to unfold, to manifest in awareness, and to express itself. To do this, the ego needs to let go of judgments about not being perfect, about not being evolved, about not being good, about not being rational, and so forth. The ego needs to understand that accepting and dealing with the lower self is an important prerequisite to spiritual growth.

In this meditation, the ego needs to affirm its commitment to reach down deep inside, to affirm that it is ready to bring the negativity and destructiveness of the lower self out into the light to be healed. The ego additionally needs to desire to examine and take responsibility for the circumstances of your life—not to blame or focus on the wrongs of others. To accomplish this, the ego must be committed to looking in detail at the antisocial desires, at the convictions, at the attitudes, and other aspects of the lower self.

The ego also looks in the other direction, toward the higher self, for guidance and wisdom. The ego should ask for assistance from both God and your spirit guides. These higher powers should be called on to help expose the destructive lower self, to help overcome resistance to spiritual growth, and to help see the lower self in a true light. These higher powers should be asked to assist in neither aggrandizing the lower self and making it into a monster, nor minimizing the lower self and writing it off as inconsequential.

As the lower self is revealed in an inner dialog mediated by the ego, the ego should probe deeper, looking for the origins of misconceptions, erroneous beliefs, and other misperceptions that may be causing negative and unpleasant manifestations in your life. When these misperceptions are recognized, guilt and self-hate will diminish proportionately. This, in turn, will encourage you to go deeper with the process.

Once the false beliefs, stubborn resistance, spitefulness, and related lower-self attributes are clearly seen for what they are, then the meditation moves into a second phase. In this phase the lower self is reoriented and reeducated. This second phase cannot take place unless you are fully aware of every aspect of the lower self's beliefs and attitudes as they relate to the troublesome circumstances in your life. In this phase you will move into a more integrated and unified place where you not only accept yourself more, but you also see what part of you needs to change in order for your life to change.

As you progressively see more of the truth about your-self, and as you commit yourself to the revelation of this truth, you will gradually perceive the greatness of your inner being, your higher self. You will come to see how you can embrace the lower self without losing sight of your innate value. In this third phase of the meditation, you see how you beat yourself up, how you have been hopeless, how you have capitulated in an effort to get what you wanted, and so forth. You will be able to let all of these things into your consciousness without diminishing your sense of yourself as a manifestation of God. This third phase happens on its own, and the ego does not need to be actively engaged in the shift to the third phase of the meditation.

In overall terms, this meditation can be conducted in silence when you are alone, or it can be conducted while writing in a personal journal. The meditation can also be accomplished with the assistance of a trusted third party, who acts as the record keeper, writing down the essential parts of your inner dialog that you then speak aloud. This type of mediation takes a good deal of time, and your patience and perseverance will pay off. You can come back to it repeatedly to go deeper with the same issues and troubles.

About the Author

Charles Cresson Wood is a Pathwork Helper based in Sausalito, California. He has a private counseling practice working with people on a wide variety of psychological and spiritual issues, including abundance concerns. Charles is additionally an Assistant Teacher on the faculty with the Pathwork of California. He has also served three terms on the board of directors for the Pathwork of California. He discovered the Pathwork in 1991 while experiencing what the Buddhists call a "dark night of the soul." At that time, he was simultaneously going through a bankruptcy, the demise of a small software firm he and his ex-wife had worked on for years, and a gut-wrenching legally contested divorce. Like many other people, he needed painful circumstances to wake up and appreciate the importance of his spiritual life. Since he began working with the Pathwork transformational process, his attitude about life, his social life, and his financial circumstances have all been dramatically transformed. In gratitude for these amazing and unanticipated changes, he has written this book.

Charles holds a bachelor of business administration degree with a major in accounting, a master of business administration degree with a major in finance, and a master of science degree with a major in computer science (all from University of Pennsylvania). He has discovered that the spiritual aspects of abundance are far more important than the rules and methodologies of money management. Unfortunately, the study of abundance in modern universities and colleges is concerned almost exclusively with the latter. Separately, Charles has published six books and over 275 technical articles dealing with information systems security and privacy. You may contact him directly at ccwood@ix.netcom.com.

This book is dedicated to
Andi, for her vision of what could be

Acknowledgments

The support of the following people is gratefully acknowledged: Gregory Alper, Simon Bailey, Chuck and Beverly Barnes, Jessica Benson, Rosalie Chamberlain, Shirley Cox Harty, Barbara Azzara, Alison Greene-Barton, Kathy Fleisher, Bob Greywolf, Deborah Holmes, Gene Humphrey, Lea Itkin, Dimitri and Catherine Karas, Andi Kiva, Maria Krekeler, Regan McCarthy, John Morrison, Brian O'Donnell, Jan Rigsby, Cecilia Sakai, Don Schramm, Sue Sherman, Bonnie Sparling, Carolyn Tilove, Dottie Titus, and Maurice Zilber. All of these people provided abundance stories for this book. All of the stories described in this book are true and accurate to the best of the author's knowledge. The names used in the stories have been changed to preserve the privacy of the contributors. Separately, thanks to Gene Humphrey and Tom Hubbard for their assistance with the editing, marketing, and positioning of this book. Thanks also to Jeff Fishel for his support in the editing of the manuscript.

Most importantly, I wish to thank Eva Broch Pierrakos for her dedicated role in the compilation of the Pathwork lecture materials that are quoted at the beginning of each day. Readers wishing to obtain the full lectures, without charge, can direct their browser to http://www.pathwork.org.

Pathwork Publications

Complete Lectures of the Pathwork
by Eva Pierrakos

The CD program of all the Pathwork lectures, including two editions—one, a minimally edited version of the originals; the second, the lectures and question and answer sessions edited for clarity and current English usage. Includes autobiographical and additional teaching material from Eva.

Pathwork Press, 2000
ISBN 0-9614777-6-8
U.S. $100.00

Pathwork Audiotape Series
by Eva Pierrakos

The original, unabridged recordings of Eva transmitting the Pathwork lectures. This is a partial listing of the titles available:

Shame of the Higher Self
Lecture 66
ISBN 1-931589-00-3
U.S. $9.95

Function of the Ego in Relation to the Real Self
Lecture 132
ISBN 1-931589-01-1
U.S. $9.95

The Process of Meditation
Lecture 182
ISBN 1-931589-02-X
U.S. $9.95

The Spiritual Meaning of Crisis
Lecture 183
ISBN 1-931589-03-8
U.S. $9.95

Identification and Intentionality
Lecture 195
ISBN 1-931589-05-4
U.S. $9.95

What is the Path?
Lecture 204
ISBN 1-931589-05-4
U.S. $9.95

The Spiritual Symbolism and Significance of Sexuality
Lecture 207
ISBN 1-931589-07-0
U.S. $ 9.95

The Spiritual and Practical Meaning of 'Let Go, Let God'
Lecture 213
ISBN 1-931589-07-0
U.S. $9.95

The Power of the Word
Lecture 233
ISBN 1-931589-07-0
U.S. $ 9.95

The Pathwork of Self-Transformation
by Eva Pierrakos

"A useful trail guide for any individual who has chosen the path of genuine spiritual growth."
—*D. Patrick Miller*, Yoga Journal

A selection of the essential guided lectures given by Eva Pierrakos. Outlines the entire Pathwork process of spiritual development, including teachings on how to transform the negativity that blocks personal and spiritual evolution. A practical, rational, and honest way to reach our deepest creativity. Edited by Judith Saly.

Bantam, 1990.
ISBN 0-553-34896-5, 282 pgs, 5⅛ x 8¼
U.S. $13.95

Fear No Evil
The Pathwork Method of Transforming the Lower Self

by Eva Pierrakos and Donovan Thesenga

"*Fear No Evil* can help us face our negative life experiences with a new light of understanding that will transform our personal pain into joy and pleasure."
—Barbara Brennan, author of
Hands of Light and *Light Emerging*

Fear No Evil offers a practical method of compassionately observing and transforming our shadow side.

Pathwork Press, 1993.
ISBN 0-9614777-2-5, 296 pgs, 5½ x 8¼
U.S. $17.95

Creating Union
The Essence of Intimate Relationship
by Eva Pierrakos and Judith Saly

"A basic primer for all of us in relationship"
— Barbara Brennan, author of *Hands of Light*

Creating Union challenges us to courageously undertake the greatest adventure of life, the journey into fearless loving and self-realization with a kindred spirit. This book compassionately answers practical questions about love, sexuality and spirituality, divorce, fear of intimacy, creating mutuality, and how to keep the spark of eros alive.

Pathwork Press, 2002.
ISBN 0-9614777-8-4, 218 pgs, 5½ x 8¼
U.S. $14.95

The Undefended Self
Living the Pathwork
Third Edition
by Susan Thesenga
based on material created by Eva Pierrakos

"A penetrating and highly effective guide in the psychological and spiritual search into the fundamental questions of life."
— *Leading Edge Review*

A profound and pragmatic guide to living the spiritual-psychological path (the Pathwork) to the undefended self, where we can no longer deny the presence of either evil or God within us. Includes true stories of people turning lifelong problems into occasions for positive movement and growth.

Pathwork Press, 2001
ISBN 0-9614777-7-6, 352 pgs, 6 x 9
U.S. $19.95

Surrender to God Within
Pathwork at the Soul Level
by Eva Pierrakos and Donovan Thesenga

"*Surrender to God Within* honors the absolutely essential step beyond an examined self into a divinely directed life, and offers not only hope and promise but the path that can take you there."
— Pat Rodegast, author of the *Emmanuel* books

Takes us beyond personal growth into the deeper questions of life's meaning and reality.

Pathwork Press, 1997
ISBN 0-9614777-5-X, 216 pgs, 6 x 9
U.S. $14.95

Pathwork Press books, tapes, and CD can be purchased through your local bookstore, through the Pathwork Press or through the Pathwork center nearest you.

Pathwork Press
P.O. Box 6010
Charlottesville, VA 22906
Phone (800) 728-4967; fax 434-817-2661
Email: pathworkpress@pathwork.org

Visit the Pathwork website at http://www.pathwork.org